IRISH ECCENTRICS

IRISH ECCENTRICS

AUBREY MALONE

First published February 2025

© Aubrey Malone
The author asserts his moral right to be identified as the author of the work.
All rights reserved. No part of this publication may be reproduced, stored in a retrieval system or transmitted in any form or by any means, electronic, mechanical, photocopying, recording or otherwise, without the prior permission of the publishers

ISBN 978-1-913144-68-5

Cover:

PENNILESS PRESS PUBLICATIONS
Website:www.pennilesspress.co.uk/books

IRISH ECCENTRICS

Adams, Gerry (1948-)
Kept the ring-pull of a hand grenade thrown at him so he could use it as a key-ring.

Agnew, David
Was offered a thousand camels for his wife, Twink, by a man in Egypt one time. The man already had four wives.

Ahern, Bertie (1951-)
Once said Charlie Haughey wanted to transform Temple Bar into Ireland's West Bank.

Believed shelving pay increases during Ireland's boom would have been 'playing smoke and Once said Charlie Haughey wanted to transform Temple Bar into Ireland's West Bank.

Believed shelving pay increases during Ireland's boom would have been 'playing smoke and daggers' with the public.

Reasoned his way out of a slip of the tongue with the following pronouncement: 'If I said it I wasn't correct. I can't recall if I did say it but I didn't say it and if I did say it I didn't mean to say it.'

At the Mahon Tribunal in 2007 he said, 'The reason I can't give you a better reflection of what I was doing on January 19 was because I wasn't doing it.'

Other 'Bertieisms' include, 'Let's not upset the apple tart', 'Hindsight is always 50-50', 'It doesn't help to throw red herrings and white elephants at each other' and 'We're not going to hang anyone on the guillotine.'

Aldridge, John (1958-)
Once speculated, 'There's only one club in Europe you can leave Manchester United for – Barcelona or Real Madrid.'

Allen, Dave (1936-2005)
Didn't like to be described as 'The comedian with half a finger.' Preferred to say, 'I'm the comedian with 9½ fingers.'

Said he was 'a paranoid in reverse'; 'I suspect people of plotting to make me happy.'

Once saw a door that had a sign on it saying, 'This door is not an entrance or an exit.' It must have been an Irish door, he concluded.

Saw another notice one day on a window that said, 'Ears Pierced While You Wait.'

'Schools these days have green blackboards,' he said. 'Why don't they just call them greenboards?'

His wife gave him two neckties as gifts one Christmas. When he came downstairs the next morning wearing one of them, she said, 'What was wrong with the other one?'

Said he wouldn't like to be offered Holy Communion from a Chinese Pope because he'd probably say, 'Will you have this here or do you want to take it away?'

Said he lost his finger when his father cut it off to punish him for picking his nose.

Likened those of a religious persuasion to people who were blindfolded in a dark room looking for a black cat that isn't there. 'And they've found it.'

Once attended a funeral and asked one of the mourners who died. 'The fella in the box,' he said.

Believed there was so much bad food going around these days, the only way to stay healthy was to starve yourself. At least that way you wouldn't die of anything serious.

Went into a pub once and the barman said they were closed. 'How did I get in then?' he asked.

Believed women were wearing dresses so short these days they'd soon have four cheeks to powder.

When he heard that, because of the population explosion, certain organisations were recycling green condoms, advised: 'Never wear one of them in the kitchen while your wife is doing the vegetables.'

Liked Ireland, he said, because it was 'the only country in the world where procrastination took on a sense of urgency.'

Always said he believed in married priests. 'If one priest loves another one,' he said, 'why shouldn't they be allowed to tie the knot?'

Felt the concept of heaven showed God to be insane: 'Why would someone make an invisible place and then put a wall around it?'

Andrews, Niall
Said U2 were his father's heroes – but he hated their music.

Asgill, John (1659-1738)
Politician who wrote a pamphlet in 1700 which proved that death wasn't obligatory for Christians. To his amazement, it caused an outcry that resulted in his expulsion from the Irish House of Commons in 1703.

The Bachelors
This musical group used to say, 'The reason we're called The Bachelors is because we're all married.'

Badmus, Ekumdayo
Represented Ireland at the World Monopoly Championships in Toronto in 200. He was born in Nigeria but wanted to sound more Irish so re-christened himself Ekumdayo O'Badmus lest there be any doubt about his nationality. To top it off, he also brought two squares of turf to the event.

Baker, Don (1950-)
Ireland's foremost harmonica player also became addicted to the guitar after he took up that instrument. So much so, in fact that he dragged his tutor off a football pitch one time during a match so that he could tune it for him. His first one was self-made fashioned from a plastic toy to which he affixed strings from a catgut tennis racquet.

Busked in Heidelberg as a young man. He took a glass of schnapps too many after one gig and climbed onto the top of a parked Volkswagen to continue the 'concert'. When its owner came upon the scene he refused to come down so he drove down the streets of the town with Don still on top of it, playing blues to his heart's content.

Ballagh, Robert (1943-)
Was described by Joseph O'Connor as 'the man who's always painting his penis.'

Banville, John (1945-)
Spent six months on a paragraph when writing one of his books.

Wrote eleven different versions of his first novel, 'Nightspawn'. Describes the muse as being like a monster that has him by the throat. Says he writes only to get such a monster to take its claws off him.

Believes he writes 24 hours a day, even while he's sleeping – because everything that ends up on a page has to pass through the mind, conscious and unconscious.

Wrote a novel called The Newton Letters in which Newton doesn't appear.

An author who describes himself as being 'terminally bored' from the ages of 7 to 17, he spent many of his childhood years walking his dog across the Wexford fields conducting imaginary interviews with himself. 'I always came off best in them,' he allows.

Feels so dissatisfied with his work to date that whenever he's passing a bookshop he wishes he could flick his fingers and magically make all his books disappear.

Barnacle, Nora (1884-1951)
Though married to James Joyce, this lady didn't have much of a clue what his books were about. Always thought he'd have made a better singer than writer.

When he copied some notes from a draft of one of his novels onto a manuscript page, she asked, 'Will all that paper be wasted now?'

Both she and her mother wrote almost totally without punctuation, which was probably the inspiration behind the style of Molly Bloom's famous soliloquy. When scholars asked Nora if she was based on Molly, she always gave the same answer: 'No. She was much fatter than me.'

When her husband's drinking went out of control, Nora used a threat against him that she knew would work: If he didn't stop, she'd have their children baptised. It worked.

Bartley, John
Belfast barrister who explained the difference between a Calvinist and a Presbyterian like this: 'A Calvinist believes all Catholics will be damned because they're predestined to be so, whereas a Presbyterian believes they'll be damned on their merits.'

Beckett, Samuel (1906-89)
A lifelong recluse, Beckett hated leaving his house even to buy a stamp. Often spent hours in people's company without uttering a word.

Believed God's only excuse for the state of the world was that he didn't exist.

Had no idea who Godot was. 'If I had, I would have said so in the play.'

Said he had no bone to pick with graveyards.

Believed if people weren't born mad they'd probably go insane.

Claimed he had memories of a foetal existence 'where no-one could free me from this agony and darkness I was subjected to.' He said he had a memory of being inside his mother's womb as she sat down to dinner with friends one day and indulged in boring tittle tattle with them. Another feeling he had was one of being assassinated before birth.

Once wrote a play that lasted for a mere 35 seconds. Entitled 'Breath', the whole text consists of precisely that emanation.

Preferred nightmares to insomnia.

Didn't give interviews 'because I have no views to inter.'

When someone told him the tramps in Waiting for Godot spoke as if they'd been to university he said, 'How do you know they haven't?'

Was unimpressed with the intellectual level of the students he taught at Campbell College in Belfast during his brief stint there as a lecturer. Informed that they were the cream of the Ulster he replied, 'Yes – rich and thick.'

Claimed to have been born on Friday 13th of April 1906, which was also Good Friday – a date that seemed to sit fittingly with his dark murmurings. His birth certificate, however, indicates he came into the world a month later.

After being stabbed by pimp Jules Prudent in 1937 he told James Joyce, who visited him in hospital, that he was much more concerned about the damage done to his coat than his perforated lung. He didn't press charges against his assailant, but wanted the judge to provide him with a new coat.

When he was directing a play once, he felt an actor hadn't dwelt long enough on a pause his stage directions indicated. He said to him, 'You're playing two dots at the moment. The script says three.'

Came out of a restaurant one day with a friend to see the sun splitting the stones. His friend said, 'A day like this makes you feel good to be alive, doesn't it?' Beckett thought for a moment and then said, 'I wouldn't go quite so far as that.'

When a fan of his work said to him, 'Mr Beckett, I've been reading your plays all my life,' Beckett replied, 'You must be very tired.'

Died in December 1989. Asked for his headstone to be 'Any colour as long as it's grey.'

Behan, Brendan (1923-64)
When he was asked how many children he and his wife had, he replied, 'Just one – me.'

He was sentenced to 14 years in prison for shooting at a detective as a young man. He said he deserved his sentence... for missing the detective. He missed him by 14 yards, so said he was doing a year for every yard: a proper punishment for his inaccuracy to his way of thinking.

Said he never came across a situation so bad that a policeman couldn't make it worse. Claimed he wanted to be one himself one time but was rejected when they found out his parents were married.

When he went to productions of his plays, often nudged the person in the seat next to him an cooed, 'I wrote that, you know.' Often became so obstreperous at rehearsals – roaring abuse at the actors – that he had to be removed.

Wrote this letter to his Hutchinson publisher Iain Hutchinson apropos a book he was working on: 'I sat at the typewriter till 8pm without eating or drinking till I finished the job. I can't drink if I'm working because it will be rubbish and I can't eat because I haven't been drinking.'

When a black man said he thought he understood the negro problem very well he replied, 'Why shouldn't I? I'm one myself.'

Asked a man one time why he hadn't fought in the Irish Uprising, 'It was over when I was born,' the man told him. Behan gave him a hard look and said, 'Excuses, excuses.'

Referred to Kiltiernan as 'the healthiest graveyard in Dublin' because it was near the sea.

When he met Norman Mailer in America, Mailer asked him if he usually had a police escort when he ventured out in public in Ireland. 'Yes,' replied Behan, 'but I'm usually handcuffed to them.'

Always carried gelignite when he was working for the IRA because, as he put it, dynamite wasn't safe.

Said he ruined his health by drinking to that of others.

Wrote a song about Michael Collins once but never sang it because 'I can never remember anything I write myself.'

After The Hostage was banned, decided to set up his own Censorship Board and censor censors.

A magistrate said to him once, 'How did you get into England in the first place?' Behan replied, 'My grandfather had an umbrella with powerful ribs on it. We were flying over London and I said to the pilot, 'Let me out here.' So he slides back the door, I opened the brolly and out I stepped.'

His mother had to leave a rooming-house when she was pregnant with him due to lack of funds. 'I'm the only writer who was ever evicted before he was born,' he boasted.

Professed not to like culchies. Met a Corkman one day and said to him, 'You don't sound like a Dub. Come back to me when you're born in Dublin.'

Was asked to come up with an advertising slogan for Guinness once. His suggestion was straightforward: 'It makes you drunk.'

Taught a cat to give an IRA salute one day by standing it on its hind legs.

Was court-martialled in his absence and sentenced to death in his absence so told them they could shoot him in his absence as well.

When he was in prison he actually 'smoked' The Bible – by putting a piece of mattress between two of its pages, lighting it and inhaling the aroma.

His diet was mainly liquid. When he bought solid food he stored it in his bathtub. One was often likely to see a chicken or a sheep's head floating round there.

Said his grandmother only got out of bed to go to funerals.

Bought The Bailey pub by accident in 1995. 'I only went to the auction' he explained, 'to buy an electric toaster.'

Behan, Brian (1926-2002)
Said where were so many people in his family, he didn't sleep alone until he was married.

Joined the communist party for a time but left because he saw too many 'rich Reds'. Then he became a Trotskyite. 'My mother thought that was some kind of horse,' he said. Was even a member of the Anarchist Party but was thrown out of it. 'How can you be thrown out of the Anarchist Party?' he asked. Another member said to him, 'That's what it's for.'

Gave up marriage for Lent one year.

Once set up a shelter for distressed women, at which he presided. If they weren't distressed coming in, he said, they certainly would be going out.

Believed the only times a woman was difficult to live with were spring, summer, autumn and winter.

After Beckett wrote a play called *Breath* which consisted of twenty seconds of silence followed by a breath, Brian said hew as contemplating writing a similar one called Fart. He described Beckett generally as 'a long string of piss who won the Nobel Prize for putting a woman in a bin for two hours on stage.'

Hated funerals so much he said he wasn't even going to his own one.

Behan, Kathleen (1889-1984)
Received a gift of some teabags from an American relative one time. She didn't know what they were for so she hung them up on the wall as Christmas decorations.

When she told Brendan she'd like to see Paris before she died he said, 'You'd better hurry up. You're hardly likely to see it afterwards.'

Often went on 'strike' from housework when she felt her children weren't pulling their weight.

Beresford Henry, 3rd Marquis of Waterford (1811-59)
Was once arrested for riding too fast on his horse through one of Waterford's busy streets where people could have been hurt. At his trial he insisted on calling the horse itself as a witness, making the perfectly reasonable point that only the steed knew for sure what speed it was travelling at. (Is this what's known as 'horse sense'?) The ploy worked and he was acquitted.

Painted a policeman green one time and tied him to the railings of a Mayfair house. Another time he put a donkey in a man's bed for a prank. Rode up the stairs on his horse at the Kilkenny Hunt Clubhouse. Threatened to knock a man's two front teeth out just so he could hear him whistle.

Bergin, Patrick (1951-)
Attended a psychiatrist once in Hollywood because 'If you don't have one there, people think you're crazy.'

Best, George (1946-2006)
Soccer's first real sex symbol insisted he slept with seven women in a 24-hour period – and with a mother and daughter together on one occasion.

Best's Manchester United team-mate Denis Law became so worried about Best's drinking habits in the early 1980s that he bought him a cassette tape that professed to help people to give up alcohol by transmitting messages while they slept. Best listened to the tape with all its soothing music and comforting messages. The pair of them met up a month later at a function. 'Well,' said Law, coming up to him, 'Was the tape any help?' 'As a matter of fact, yes,' Best reassured him. 'It's stopped me drinking alright, but only when I'm asleep.'

Once played a whole game without using his right foot so he could strengthen his left one.

On another occasion he dispossessed one of his own team-mates of the ball.

Once saw a player trapping a ball with his bottom and though: 'If he can do that, so can I.' So he did.

Didn't know how to open a bank account or even do something like buy a Postal Order. 'I tried it once but ended up at the wrong counter.'

Was once asked what was the closest to a soccer kick-off that he'd had sex with a woman. 'Half time,' he replied.

Sent his son to a school that promised to make him like Bobby Charlton. He came back bald.

Discounted the rumour that he slept with seven Miss Worlds: 'I only slept with four of them. I didn't turn up for the other three.'

Said of Tommy Docherty's autobiography: 'It's one of those books that, when you put it down, you can't take it up again.'

Was in the pub one day where he was arguing about a soccer scoreline. Nobody would give way so he got a taxi back to his flat twenty miles away to check it. The fare cost more than £100.

Said he spent most of his money on women and drink – and the rest he wasted.

When he had his liver transplant he got forty pints in ten hours – which, he said, beat his previous record by about twenty minutes.

The Big O
Says his father wasn't very well educated. The first time he saw Brussels Sprouts he said, 'Who made a balls of the cabbage?'

His father couldn't afford laxatives when he was a child so he used to sit him on the po and tell him ghost stories.

Binchy, Maeve (1940-2012)
Didn't feature sex in her books because she'd never been to an orgy, had never swung from a chandelier over a coffee table and didn't know where the arms and legs would go.

Never hung up on a crossed line when on the phone because the conversations she heard there provided the raw material for much of her writing.

Probably the only person in history to lose their faith on a trip to the Holy Land. 'It looked too ordinary,' she said of the tomb where Jesus lay after being crucified.

If you lost your virginity in Ireland when she was growing up, she said, somebody would probably have found it for you and brought it back to your mother.

Fell madly in love with Marlon Brando as a young woman and kept writing him letters. Wasn't happy about the women he was dating. Wanted him to leave Hollywood and come over to Dublin so she could mind him.

Bird, Errol
This well-named gentleman is credited with the most protracted yodel on record – 10 hours and 15 minutes. The feat was achieved in Lisburn on October 6, 1979.

Bishop, Des (1975-)
The reason Irish people never mind you being late for an appointment, he suggests, is because they're not there either.

Likes putting on accents so much he even does so when he's imitating himself.

Says he learned to speak Irish by watching Al-Jazeera TV broadcasts.

Believes Taytos are Ireland's national food.

Thinks our greatest national obsession is trying not to over-use the hot press.

Blake, Joseph (1797-1849)
This former resident of Ardrey House in Galway went on to acquire the title Lord Wallscourt. He also went on to develop a habit of parading around the grounds of the house in the nude. A cowbell draped around his neck allowed any maids in the vicinity to make themselves scarce before his wobbly bits came into view.

Blanchflower, Danny (1926-93)
'The secret of football,' he remarked, 'is to equalise before the other side scores.'

Said the F.A. Cup Final was a wonderful occasion until about ten minutes to three. Then the players came on and ruined the whole thing.

Bolger, Dermot (1959-)
Decided at twelve that he wanted to be a writer but when a friend told him he might have to go to college for that he decided he might try and become a murderer instead.

One of his early books of poetry was called Leinster Street Ghosts. 'It was really nine novels, two films and a play in twelve pages,' he explains.

Bonner, Ted (1917-2002)
Took his car to a garage to have the brakes fixed. The mechanic couldn't manage that, however. 'I made the horn louder instead,' he offered.

Bono (1960-)
Is reputed to have difficulty combing his hair without scratching his halo, and to have written 'Manger' on his passport once under 'Place of Birth'.

Lists 1978 as U2's most exciting year. 'It was then we discovered a fourth chord. We only had three up till then.'

Was on a plane with Sophia Loren one time when it was struck by lightning. 'Don't worry,' he assured her, 'That's just God taking your photograph.'

Started writing the album *War* on his honeymoon.

When asked what was the main thing that kept U2 from disbanding over the years, he replied, 'Fear of our manager.'

Bowen, Elizabeth (1899-1973)
Liked Italian graves because they looked 'more lived in' than Irish ones.

Boylan, Sean (1949-)
Went into Terry Brady's shop in Fairyhouse some years ago for a bun and came out with a motorised buggy. Another day he went in for an ice cream and came out with a chainsaw.

Boyle, Robert (1627-91)
In 1680 this scientist published a paper documenting how one could make phosphorous by heating urine with sand.

Bowman, John
Says he often gets letters from people when he calls Galway a town, which he never does.

Brady, Liam (1956-)
Said of a reliable goalkeeper: 'He hasn't made any saves you wouldn't have expected him not to make.'

Brannagh, Kenneth (1960-)
His parents didn't mind him living with a girl before he was married, consoling themselves with the fact it meant he would probably eat better.

Branigan, James 'Lugs' (1910-86)
A colourful combination of Clint Eastwood's 'Dirty Harry' and Sylvester Stallone's Rocky Balboa, this two-fisted ex-boxer was a policeman with a difference. When he arrested people, he usually offered them the choice of a night behind bars or a punch in the face. One thing was sure, if they plumped for the latter option, it cut down on paperwork – or the need for a solicitor.

'Lugs' frequently beat people to a pulp on the street, and received grudging approval for this. One mother of a juvenile delinquent said, 'Mr Branigan always got a cup of tea before he lagged one of my boys.'

Also waged war on Dublin's red light district but knew where to stop. When he retired, he received a canteen of cutlery from the whip-round of a set of prostitutes.

Once sat on a man to subdue him. The man bit him on the rear end, causing Lugs to remark, 'He was worse than the Balubas. At least they cook you first.'

Breen, Kieran
Roscrea boy who got a prosthetic leg as a result of a disability in 2006. According to his mother Sonia he has to report to the HSE every 18 months to assure them he hasn't grown a new natural one.

Brenan, John (1768-1830)
Quack doctor who imagined turpentine cured almost every ailment. Was fired from the Rotunda Hospital for prescribing it during an epidemic of puerperal (i.e. child-bed) fever. Was also into wrestling. Frequently broke his opponent's shins and then offered to treat them. With turpentine.

Brennan, Shay (1937-2000)
The late football international was asked how he spent his time when he wasn't playing football. He replied, 'Walking into glass doors, dipping my tie into soup bowls, going to the loo at functions and ending up at the wrong function upon my return.'

Broe, Ken (1973-)
Bouncer who bit off part of a man's ear in 2007. He had eight previous convictions. His defence was that he was depressed over recently being diagnosed as having Mad Cow Disease.

Brown, Christy (1932-81)
When his father told him God made everything in the world he called him a liar because his father had previously told him only bricklayers could build houses and he knew God wasn't a bricklayer.

Browne, Dermot
Jockey who was arrested for doping horses in 2011. One commentator remarked, 'Why wasn't the horse arrested? He was the one taking the dope after all, wasn't he?'

Burke, Seamus (1888- ?)
Burke was a Kilkenny man who became an enterologist – as opposed to an escapologist. One of his stunts involved getting into a trunk that was locked and encircled with rope

without breaking a wax seal. In another one he had himself tied to a chair with a sealed bag placed over his shoulders. He managed to escape from his bondage, put himself into the bag and re-tie himself to the chair while inside it.

Butler, Tony
Believed the Irish climate was wonderful but the weather ruined it.

Heard a clergyman in Portadown telling his congregation one Sunday afternoon, 'If you were here this morning to see the empty seats you'd have been ashamed of yourselves for staying away.'

Described an Irish alibi as proof that someone was in two places at the one time.

Knew a man whose alibi for not committing a particular crime was that he was 'nowhere at all' on the night in question.

Said of a condemned criminal: 'He'd been sentenced to death but he saved his life by dying in jail.'

Byrne, Ed (1972-)
Says he's so pessimistic he's even pessimistic about the pessimism of other pessimists.

Doesn't like pornographic films because he can never follow the plots.

Byrne, Gabriel (1950-)
During the four years he spent studying to be a priest he developed a penchant for guzzling altar wine and chewing on congealed candle grease.

A woman asked him for his autograph one day. 'What name will I put on it?' he asked. 'Your own', she replied.

Was present at the birth of his son by Ellen Barkin. He wasn't looking forward to it so asked the doctor in charge if the maternity room had a window with a good view. The doctor said it was the first time he'd been asked such a question in 34 years of practice.

Said his daughter went to her room one day after dinner when she was twelve and didn't come out till she was 21.

Sees the main achievement of his film career as managing to rape King Arthur's mother in Excalibur while wearing a full suit of armour.

Edited a literary magazine when he was at UCD. Wrote a lot of stories under pseudonyms to give the impression the magazine had more contributors than it had. Made up biographies for these pseudonyms like, 'Seam Mac Chommaraigh was born in the Donegal gaeltacht in 1953 and is at present serving in a ministerial capacity in Ghana.'

Says he went to Spain for the Civil War but arrived about 35 years too late so decided to teach English in Bilbao instead.

Was once propositioned by an elderly plumber with emphysema who offered him two and six for a look at his privates.

Byrne, Gay
The workaholic broadcaster interviewed everyone from presidents to famous actors to world champion sports people but still said what he was most proud of is the fact that one

day a woman went into his garden in Howth and kissed his bin.

When he was doing his radio show he said to a caller on the phone, 'What are you doing now?' She replied, 'Talking to you.'

After he was defrauded by Russell Murphy, developed temporary paralysis in his hand every time he tried to write a cheque. 'My hands just wouldn't move across the page,' he said.

Byrne, Jason (1972-)
Admits that his child is a 'bit deranged.' Because he lives with his father.

He says he came from a poor family: 'My mother used to ask the butcher for a bone even though we had no dog. We were fed on a diet of lamb's hearts and livers.'

As his mother gets older, he tells us, she also gets smaller. As a result of this, he doesn't believe she'll ever die. She'll just disappear.

Byrne, Mary (1959-)
Went to a party with so many famous people one night 'I was the only one I never heard of.'

Campbell, Liam
After giving the details of a competition once, the radio DJ said, 'Send your answers on a postcard. The winner will be the first one opened.'

Campbell, Patrick
Stammered so much he wasn't able to say the word 'stammer' without stammering.

Said his feet were size ten and sideways size twelve. 'They're round like an elephant's,' he explained.

Cameron, Sir Charles (1830-1921)
Dublin Doctor who tried to help the city's sanitary conditions in 1911. There was a particularly hot summer that year and Cameron offered people threepence for every bag of dead flies they collected. The catch was that the bags were so big, over 6000 flies were needed to fill each one. not many people took up the offer.

Carelli, Patrick
Alleged to have drunk a pint of stout in less than three seconds at Keelings pub in Donabate, Dublin, in March 2001.

Carey, Sarah
Spotted a driver one day negotiating a roundabout with a phone in one hand and a take-out coffee in the other. She was steering the car with her elbows.

Carmody, Dermot
This comedian said he only started acting Irish since he emigrated to England: 'Back home there didn't seem much point.'

Carpenter, Holly (1991-)
Once sent a text to her best friend to tell him she wasn't talking to him.

Carr, Jimmy (1972-)
Agrees that boxers shouldn't have sex the night before a fight – especially if they don't fancy each other.

As a New Man, says he has no problem buying tampons for women but unfortunately they don't seem to regard them as proper presents.

Thinks the road sign, 'Slow – Children's School' is offensive. On the other hand, if they're slow enough they won't be able to understand it.

Dates his first midlife crisis from the age of 26.

Childers, Erskine (1870-1922)
Refused a blindfold when he was being executed by the British in 1922 for his IRA activities. Shook hands with his executioners and even said to them before they shot him, 'Step a little closer, boys, it will be easier for you that way.'

Carr, Roddy
Said of the golfer Vincente Fernandez: 'He walks with a slight limp. This is because he was born with one leg shorter than the other two.'

Carson, Frank (1926-2012)
When he was young, a classmate of his was asked to describe a lift to his teacher. 'It's like this,' he said, 'You go into a wee room and when you shut the door on yourself, the upstairs comes down on top of ye.'

Claimed he once sold furniture for a living. 'The only problem was that it was my own.'

Thieves broke into his local chemist and stole everything but contraceptives and Brylcreem. Police immediately mounted a search for a bald-headed Catholic.

Once saw this ad in a Belfast newspaper: 'Wanted: Man and woman to look after two cows, both Protestant.'

Loved marriage. It was his wife he couldn't stand.

Didn't think his wife liked him very much. After he had a heart attack, she *wrote* for an ambulance.

Met Pope Benedict towards the end of his life. The Pope asked him if he'd ever met Elvis Presley. He replied, 'No, but it won't be long before I do.'

Cascarino, Tony (1962-)
Described a fellow player who didn't impress him as 'not the sharpest sandwich in the picnic.'

Cleary, Bridget (? – 1895)
Tipperary woman killed by her husband and some other men who suspected her of being a witch. After Bridget became ill in 1895 her husband Michael suspected it wasn't his wife who was in the sick bed at all. He thought she'd been abducted by fairies and a changeling left in her place. He dragged her over to a fire to burn the alien presence out of her and she died in the blaze. He was convicted of manslaughter and served fifteen years in prison. Bridget came to be known as 'The last witch burned in Ireland', but some sceptics believe Michael killed her because he was jealous of her – she was an independent woman who owned one of the first Singer sewing machines in Ireland – and resentful of the fact that she hadn't given him any children

after eight years of marriage. The case gave rise to a nursery rhyme:
'Are you a witch or are you a fairy
Or are you the wife of Michael Cleary?'

Coffee, John
Built a jail in Dundalk in 1953. Became its first inmate for nonpayment of debts after he became bankrupt during its construction. 'If I hadn't built it so well,' he remarked wryly from behind bars, 'I could probably have escaped.'

Coleman, Edwin
This farmer was fined for selling a calf in Tullow in 2002 without giving the buyer its passport. 'I had no intention it wished to travel,' he remarked after the sentence was passed.

Colgan, Michael (1950-)
Described the Gate Theatre as his mistress.

Coll, Vincent (1908-32)
This Gweedore-born gentleman was raised in the Bronx. Rather early on in life he cottoned on to the genius of kidnapping gangsters and seeking ransoms for release, on the basis that their families would hardly go to the police, nor release details of any ransom payments to the taxman. The mayor of New York, Jimmy Walker, dubbed him 'Mad Dog' but not even a man this tough could escape a hood's bullet forever and he stopped one of these on February 8, 1932.

Collins, Michael (1890-1922)
Collins was often asked how he'd eluded capture by the British for so long. 'Because I never assume anything,' was his reply. One day in 1914 he was on a train with a colleague when they spotted a flock of sheep. 'They've just been

shorn,' said the colleague. 'At least on this side,' Collins replied.

Connaughton, Shane (1941-)
Believes Jesus was Irish. 'He was unmarried after all, he lived at home until he was thirty and his mother thought he was God.'

Connery, Donald S.
Believed that while the rest of the world would say a problem was serious but not impossible, an Irishman would say, 'It's impossible but not very serious.'

Connolly, John (1968-)
After getting a £35,000 advance for his novel Every Dead Thing he said his first priority was to fix the heater in his car.

Says he didn't have an unhappy childhood but was an unhappy child.

Connors, Shaun
Dressed in his father's hand-me-downs as a child. One pair of trousers were so big he had to open the fly to blow his nose.

Has a friend who bought a microwave television. He can now watch a three-hour film in five minutes.

Heard about a new contraceptive pill designed specially for Catholics. It weighs three tons. Women roll it up against the bedroom door so their husbands can't get in.

Cook, Robert (1644-1726)
This 17th century farmer from Waterford was such an animal lover that he even refused to kill foxes that attacked his poultry. When a fox killed a chicken he owned once, he took it aside and did his best to explain to it that the Fifth Commandment forbade such barbarity. The fox must have taken his advice on board because it departed peacefully.

Cook always wore white. Not only were his shirts and nightclothes that colour but also his suits, coats and hats. He even insisted his horses and cattle be white. Not surprisingly, his soubriquet was 'Linen Cook'. He was buried in a white shroud.

Cooke, Adolphus (1792-1876)
Landowner who also saw huge links between the human and animal worlds. If anything, he treated animals more seriously. One day he got so annoyed with his dog, Gusty, for wandering he 'arrested' and then put him on trial. The jury deliberated for hours before returning a verdict of guilty. Adolphus then passed a sentence of death upon the unfortunate dog. He ordered him to be hanged and prepared a headstone that said, 'Executed for high crimes and misdemeanours, Gusty. It is earnestly hoped that his sad fate will be a warning to other dogs against so offending.' A hangman was duly appointed to do the dastardly deed but as he knotted the rope the dog began speaking to him 'in some kind of foreign language' as he put it, and he desisted. Augustus appreciated his decision and allowed Gusty to live to a ripe old age.

When he saw one of his bullocks in danger of drowning in a local river he brought all his other cattle down to the bank to watch it so they'd learn from his mistakes and 'shun water during their mortal tenure.'

Believed his father was reincarnated as a turkey cock he kept in his grounds. Men had to doff their heads to this when they passed it, and women to genuflect.

Believed he would be reincarnated as a fox himself. Asked his servants to dig numerous foxholes on his grounds which he expected to use when the time came. Such foxholes were gigantic constructions large enough to contain a table and chairs from which he could write his posthumous memoirs – presumably with his feet.

Hated children so much he once gave a beggar £5 merely because he was childless.

Cosgrave, Liam (1920-)
The former Taoiseach believed Jews and Muslims should settle their differences in accordance with Christian principles.

Costello, Joe (1945-)
This politician had an unusual electioneering style. He kissed the mothers and shook hands with the babies.

Crampton, Sir Philip (1777-1858)
This surgeon picked an unusual topic for his doctoral thesis: the construction of birds' eyes.

Had a horror of being eaten by rats after he died. Asked to be buried in cement as a preventative measure.

Crickett, Jimmy (1945-)
Went to see *The Ten Commandments* once. Before it was over, he said, the couple in the seat behind him had broken five of them.

Says he's eaten so many fish in his life, his stomach goes in and out with the tide.

Tried to drown himself one day but failed: 'The goldfish wouldn't move over.'

Says he used to know a priest who had stained glass lenses in his glasses.

Got a job in a hardware shop. A man came in and said he wanted some nails. Cricket asked him how long he wanted them. The man said, 'I want to keep them.'

Cruise, Jack (1915-79)
Knew a man who was so industrious he went on his honeymoon alone, leaving his wife to mind the shop.

Was always glad he wasn't born in Italy because he didn't speak a word of Italian.

Cuddy, Joe
When his wife told him she was 'sick of looking at the four walls' he knocked one of them down.

Knew a man who was dating a twin. 'How do you tell the difference?' he asked him. 'It's easy,' the man replied, 'Her brother has a moustache.'

Said the town he came from was so small, the local fire brigade was a 10-year-old bed-wetter.

Told of a virgin who went to New York. A prostitute asked him if he wanted to sleep with her for fifty dollars. 'I'm not really tired,' he said, 'but I could do with the money.'

Says he goes to the toilet every morning at 7.30. The only problem is, he doesn't get up until 8.30.

Cullens, Michael
Thinks Padraig Harrington has a voice like Rice Krispies. Says Irishmen only cry when they're assembling Ikea furniture. Wonders why the police put photographs of criminals up in post offices. Are we supposed to write to them?

Cummins, Danny (1914-84)
Said he didn't normally sing, and when he did he didn't sing normally.

Curley, Frank
Mathematician who was once asked why he was childless, 'I can't multiply,' he confessed.

Curran, John Philpott (1750-1817)
Curran was a barrister with a rapier-like wit that wouldn't have been lost on the likes of Oscar Wilde. It was even apparent on his deathbed when his doctor remarked that he was coughing very badly. 'That's surprising,' said Curran, 'as I have been practising all night.'

Designed a unique alarm clock when he was a student. It consisted of two tin vessels which he suspended over his head at ten o'clock pm, his bedtime. He poured water into the upper one and made a tiny hole in the bottom one, so small that it took over six hours for the water to pour through. When it did, it was morning and soaked him sufficiently to wake him.

Cusack, Cyril (1910-93)
Had a reputation for upstaging his fellow actors. When Siobhan McKenna was appearing opposite him in The Cherry Orchard she was asked when auditions were starting. 'Probably soon,' she answered, 'I see Cyril is already rehearsing his cough.'

Was once heard to say, 'I don't believe in fairies even if they exist.'

Daly, K.S.
Knew a man who bought a packet of condoms in the Virgin Megastore because he was too embarrassed to get a Daniel O'Donnell record.

Davidson, Treasa
The former RTÉ continuity announcer said once, 'And now as we come to The News at 1.30 we have to leave Harry Belafonte with his hole in the bucket.'

Davis, Derek (1948-2015)
A friend of his said to him one day when it started raining. 'An hour of this will do as much good in ten minutes as a month of it would do in a fortnight at any other time of the year.'

Once said that being Irish meant driving a German car to an American-themed pub for a Belgian beer, then grabbing an Indian curry on the way home before setting on Swedish furniture to watch British programmes on Japanese TVs.

As he began to pile on the weight he confessed, 'My stomach is going on for a career of its own.'

Davitt, Michael (1846-1906)
Believed you weren't a proper member of an Irish club until you were barred.

Day-Lewis, Daniel (1957-)
Spent a brief spell as a journalist before becoming an actor. Tried to write a book review once but after reading it twice and thinking about it for three weeks, decided he had nothing to say about it so threw it aside.

After he got the part of Abraham Lincoln in 2013 he asked, 'Will I be expected to die for real in the film as a bona fide Method actor?'

Won an Oscar for that role. Meryl Streep won that year for playing Margaret Thatcher in *The Iron Lady*. Said Day-Lewis, 'They got the parts mixed up. I was supposed to play Thatcher and Meryl to play Lincoln.'

Delamere, Neil (1979-)
Says there are more cars on the road in Ireland on car-free days than anywhere else in the world. Everyone says, 'Jaysus, there'll be nothin' on the road today. I'll drive to work.'

Delaney, Patrick
Dublin doctor who was playing poker with a priest one night in the 1940s in Kildare when the priest dropped dead. The excitement of getting a straight flush was thought to be the cause. Because it would have been seen as a scandal for a priest to die while playing poker, Dr Delaney rang a cardiologist friend of his and arranged to have the corpse driven to Dublin so that a more respectable place of death could be arranged. Half way to the city, however, the car ran out of petrol. It was the middle of the night so a garage

owner in the midlands had to be woken up to fill the tank. After he had done so he wiped the sleep from his eyes and looked in the car window at the 'sinister slump' of the priest's body in the back seat, 'Jesus boys,' he said to the other passengers, 'I'm not sure I like the look of your friend.'

Dempsey, Ian (1961-)
Couldn't think of any sins to tell for his First Confession so made up one. Was then told *that* was a sin, telling a lie. That was his first experience of Catholic guilt.

De Valera, Eamon (1882-1975)
Was arrested in the middle of a speech he gave in Clare in 1918 and imprisoned for a year. When he was released he went back to the same place and began a new speech with the words, 'As I was saying before I was interrupted...'

Used to smoke turf as a young man.

Dignam, Christy (1960-)
Says of Aslan's early days, 'The first 600 refusals are the hardest.'

Doherty, Gary (1980-)
The former Irish international offered this insight on a forthcoming match: 'It's a no-win game for us, although I suppose we can win by winning.'

Doherty, Ken (1969-)
Was once beaten five-nil in a snooker match, 'and I was lucky to get nil.'

Said Fred Davis started playing snooker when the Dead Sea was only sick.

Married a psychiatrist 'because you'd need to be mad to play snooker for a living.'

Dolan, Joe (1913-2007)
Said the reason he was so popular in Israel was because he had a big nose.

Donegan, Paddy (1923-2000)
Said of Northern Ireland in 1976, 'There's no way we'll accept an acceptable level of violence.'

Dunleavy, J.P. (1928-)
Says he has a posthumous ambition to 'decompose in a barrel of porter and have it served in all the bars of Dublin.'

Donnelly, Patrick
Belfast man who found a wallet lying in the road one day. Its owner was... Patrick Donnelly. The other one lived in Augher, County Tyrone.

Donovan, James
Is a supporter of capital punishment: 'Where would Christianity be if Jesus got eight to ten years, with time off for good behaviour?'

Donovan, Patrick
Heard a charity appeal on the radio that said it only takes ten euros to support a family in Africa so is thinking of moving his whole family out there.

Doolin, Matt
Knew a man who received an item in the post which he refused to pay for. 'I never ordered it,' he wrote back to the man who sent him the invoice, 'and if I did you didn't send

it to me. if you did I never got it and if I did I already paid for it. And if I didn't, I won't.

Doonican, Val (1927-2015)
Liked golf to being with an 18-year-old girl with big boobs: 'You know it's wrong but you can't keep away from her.'

Believed the reason dogs weren't good dancers was because they had two left feet.

Asked his grand-daughter if she ever saw him on television: 'No,' she said, 'I saw you on the sofa.'

Doorley, Tom
Once got 3% in an exam. All he had right was the teacher's name.

Dowling, Brian (1978-)
Was a closet gay before he entered the Big Brother House in 2001. 'I went in to come out,' he said.

Dowling, Vincent (1929-2013)
This actor's mother had seven children by his father, whom she disliked. He said, 'It makes you wonder how many she'd have had if she liked him.'

Spent most of his life in America. Claimed he'd do anything for Ireland except live here.

Said Brian Friel always listened very carefully to his theatrical suggestions. Before rejecting them.

Once played God in a play. His wife said it was typecasting.

Doyle, Jack (1913-78)
When he was down and out in the late forties, he asked a man for money. When he was refused he lifted him up and dumped him in a workman's hole and began shovelling earth on him. The man ran for his life. Another time he pawned a friend's wooden leg for £5 when he was asleep.

In 1938 during a bout with Eddie Thompson. Doyle's enthusiasm got the better of him. After psyching himself up for a hefty punch he completely missed Thompson altogether and fell out of the ring. Knocking *himself* out.

Doyle happened to be in a hotel with his wife Movita – she was subsequently to marry Marlon Brando – when Hitler walked in accompanied by his uniformed lieutenants. Everyone stood to attention except Doyle and Movita. 'I'm Irish' he told her, 'we don't have to stand.'

Doyle, Lynn
This lady thinks the best way to live to a ripe old age is to get an ulcer when you're young. You'll be so busy taking care of yourself for fear of upsetting it, she says, you'll outlast all around you.

Doyle Roddy, (1958-)
In a week in the 1980s he did four different interviews in four different countries in four different pubs, all called The Dubliner.

Once got a letter from a woman who was compiling a book of letters from famous writers. She asked him if he had one to contribute. He wrote back to her to say he hadn't. She then wrote back to him and asked if she could use that one.

After he became famous he received a request from an anonymous businessman to endorse a green Wonderbra for the World Cup.

Liked Bob Dylan's LP 'Highway 61 Revisited' so much he played it until the batteries on his Walkman ran out. But he still doesn't know if off by heart: 'How could I? I've only been listening to it for fifty years.'

Drew, Ronnie (1934-2008)
Got married in O'Donoghue's pub. 'It made sense,' he said, 'I was seeing more of the barman than my fiancée.' O'Donoghue's was also where he mainly sang with the Dubliners.

Singing wasn't all he did. 'I went to a party there one night in 1963' he said, 'and it was still going on in 1970.'

Asked what was the best part of being in the group he said, 'The arguments. It was a strange week when someone didn't drop out.'

Met Paddy Kavanagh one day in the sixties and asked him if he'd like to go for a drink. He suggested Mooney's but Kavanagh said he was barred from there. Kavanagh then suggested Searsons but Drew couldn't go there for the same reason. Drew suggested The Clubhouse. 'No good,' Kavanagh said, 'Barred again. What about Andy Ryan's?' Drew said he was barred from there so he said, 'We better leave it. Good luck.' And they parted.

Drimmie, David
Drimmie was the Secretary of the English and Scottish Law Life Assurance Association in Tyrone in 1872. He wrote a

letter to one of his agents that year but it didn't arrive until 1910, 38 years later.

Dudley, Thomas (1906-81)
When most of us where children, we used to act out the scenarios from cowboy films after we left the cinema. What made Dudley different was the fact that he continued the practice right though his life.

Using a large golden jail key as his gun and slapping his rear end to indicate his trusty steed, he rampaged through the streets of Dublin dispensing rough justice on baddies in the absence of Ray Rogers or Hopalong Cassidy being able to do the job for real.

Dudley, who was better known as 'Bang Bang', engaged in street theatre before the term was invented. When he aimed his key at you, you had to put your hands up. When he fired it, you had to die. These were the rules of the game. Except it wasn't a game. It was real life. Because Bang Bang believed it, so did you. He caused full scale duels to erupt on buses and trams as well as in the streets. Why did so many people play along with him? Much of it was down to his intense conviction in what he was doing, right up to middle age. 'Bang, you're shot,' he'd say, 'If yeh don't die, I'm not playing,' and that scenario would have been too horrible to contemplate, so yeh did.

In his later years he became known as 'Lord' Dudley. When his eyesight started to fail, he engaged in less gunplay, though he still managed a creation of the Gunfight at the OK Corral with Johnny Fortycoats, another 'character'. 'I don't use my gun much since I became Lord Dudley,' he told Eamon Mac Thomais one day, after which he took out his key and 'shot' him. It was a good trick. He was obviously just trying to lull MacThomais into a false sense of security.

The key is still on display in the Reading Room of the Dublin City Archive in Pearse Street.

Duff, Damien (1979-)
Was so difficult to get up in the morning, his manager thought he suffered from Adhesive Mattress Syndrome.

Duffy, Joe (1956-)
Cites the biggest influence on his life as 'The Tech in Ballyfermot, which is the I *didn't* go to.'

Dunlop Anne (1968-)
Thought Northern Ireland was an island until she was twelve.

Dunne, Ben (1949-)
Asked what was the first thing he'd say to God if he got to heaven, replied, 'I've been dying to see you.'

Dunne, Mary (1928-2014)
Mary Dunne's dulcet tones rang down O'Connell Street for many years as she held court there 'singing' the rosary to anyone who stopped to listen. She may have looked like she wasn't the full shilling but if you stopped to talk to her she proved to be a real sweetie. A former schoolteacher, she gave up her retirement years to this peculiar form of evangelism. O'Connell Street was her parish, her ministry. She sang and danced till the cows came home, like a nun in mufti or a female Elmer Gantry, her extravagant garb and showy ear-rings offsetting the devoutness beautifully.

Dunphy, Eamon (1945-)
Believes Irish soccer fans always enjoy celebrating more when we lose than when we win.

Never liked the description of himself as a failed Third Division player. 'What I am is a failed *Second* Division player.'

Eamon McCann said he played football like Mario Lanza and sang like Maradona.

Eclin, Thomas
18th century Irishman (in)famous for eating live cats and dogs.

Lord Emley
Limerick peer who spent the last fifteen years of his life in bed. With the curtains drawn.

Emmet, Robert (1778-1803)
Donal Foley claimed that his head was found in 1953 by Bord Failte and was given a breathalyser test which caused it to turn a deep green. It was then rushed to the Special Criminal Court where it was accused of subversive activity. The head offered no evidence to the contrary and was sentenced to ten years in Kilmainham prison.

Enright, Anne (1962-)
Wrote one of her books rocking a cradle with one hand and typing with the other.

Wonders where the Virgin Mary goes to the toilet considering she was assumed bodily into heaven.

Says she's only a woman 'on Tuesdays.'

The only reason cats jump into your lap, she believes, is to see if you're cold enough to eat.

Fanning, Dave (1955-)
His brother won the Rooney Prize for poetry one year. When he showed him his first collection, Fanning mistook the Glossary for a poem.

Interviewed Robin Williams once. 'He's the only man I ever met who talked faster than me,' he said.

Farrell, Colin (1976-)
Movie-making is fickle, he allows. One minute you're hot, the next you're in Mexico in some turkey about cockroaches taking over the planet and telling people in some dingy bar that you used to be someone once.

One week during his substance abuse years he took 20 ecstasy tablets, 4 grams of cocaine, 6 of speed, half an ounce of hash, three bottles of Jack Daniels, 12 bottles of red wine, 60 pints of beer and 280 cigarettes. And he still felt flat.

Tried to be an atheist but 'I didn't have the faith.'

When asked what he would say to God if he met him he replied, 'I wouldn't have to say anything. He'd know what I was thinking.'

Used to leave smarties under his bed for Marilyn Munroe as a young boy. He thought they'd bring her back to life.

Johnny Farthing
Johnny was an intellectually challenged street character who loved farthings so much he used to offer people a penny for

one even though they were only valued at a quarter of that. Or maybe he was smarter than the lot of them at the back of it all. According to legend, he built up a huge collection of farthings from those who were so amused by him they let him keep the pennies as well as the farthings.

Feherty, David (1958-)
Feels one more rule needs to be added to golf: 'Players should be allowed to tackle their opponents.

Compares Jim Furyk's swing to a man trying to kill a snake in a phone box.

Sings to punish his children.

Fielding, Mark
Chief executive of ISME who complained about the number of bogus sick certs handed out to Irish workers who were serial absentees from work in 2009. Flus and bad backs were the most common excuses. Other more colourful ones included: 'I had to help deliver a baby on my way to work.' 'I drove through the automatic garage door before it opened.' 'I cut my fingernails too short and they're bleeding.' 'The ghosts in my house kept me awake last night.' 'My cow bit me.' 'My son fell asleep next to wet cement. His foot fell in and we can't get it out.' 'I forgot I was getting married today.' 'My boyfriend's snake escaped from its cage and I'm afraid to leave the bedroom till he gets home.'

Fitzgerald, F Scott (1896-1940)
The writer often 'blamed' his alcoholic excesses on his Irish background. Was known to spend a lot of his time at parties on all fours under tables, or throwing things at people, sometimes resulting in the hosts of such parties walking out

and leaving him to entertain himself in an empty room. On one occasion where he threw a party for his daughter Scottie, he ended up throwing her out and asking a band he'd employed for the evening to continue playing for him alone as he sat listening to them in the middle of a hotel room with a bottle of gin in his hand. In the course of another party he asked the guests to give him their wallets and watches, which he then put into a pot and proceeded to make soup from them.

Was so impressed with James Joyce, after he met him in Paris he threatened to throw himself out a window to express his adulation. Joyce thankfully prevailed upon him to desist.

When his wife Zelda told him his penis was too small to satisfy her, he solicited the advice of his friend Ernest Hemingway on the issue. Hemingway took him into a toilet and examined it, concluding that it was normal in size except perhaps when viewed from a height. Fitzgerald nodding approvingly at the diagnosis – though Zelda went on to accuse Hemingway and Fitzgerald of having a homosexual relationship.

Fitzgerald, Garrett (1926-2011)
Played rugby as a young man. Gave it up when he learned you had to run with the ball.

When his wife heard he'd gone out of the house with odd shoes on one day she said, 'The surprise is that he remembered to put them on at all.'

Fitzgerald, George Robert (1748-86)
The Fighting Fitzgerald, as he was known because of his ferocious temper, was descended from the Normans. He was

addicted to fighting. He grew up in Mayo but went on to serve in the British Army. One day a man brushed past him in a coffee-house with the words, 'I smell an Irishman.' Fitzgerald drew out a knife and cut his nose off. 'You shall never smell another one,' he told him.

Was shot in the skull during a Galway duel. His life was saved by an operation in which a circular saw shaved off part of his head to get at the bullet but his brain was said to be affected by the procedure. Either due to this or his own volatile nature, the following years saw various examples of outrageous behaviour.

One day he stabbed a man who accidentally stepped on his dog's foot. Another time he had his horse scale a wall with a 14-foot drop on the other side for a bet. The horse died as a result. He also shot the dog of a local aristocrat. His reason? He felt it was better fed than some of the man's servants and wanted to apprise him of that fact.

Married in 1770 and went to France on his honeymoon. Here he rode to the hounds with King Louis XV, his gigantic ego causing him to ride in front of the king. He formed an attachment to bears during this trip and brought a number of them home with him, as well as some foxes and vicious dogs. One day after an argument with his father about money he tied him to one of the bears to punish him. More spectacularly, he dressed a bear up as a person on another occasion, decking him out in a blue travelling cloak and a scarlet cape and putting him sitting next to an attorney in a coach that was going from Dublin to Mayo. 'Just welt him a little,' Fitzgerald told the attorney as he revealed his travelling companion's true identity, 'and keep him quiet until we reach Kinnegad, where we breakfast.' The attorney darted from the coach and ran for his life.

As Fitzgerald aged, the arguments with his father grew more fierce. After one of them he imprisoned him in a cave. When he was arrested for this, he became furious with his father and kidnapped him, taking him to a deserted island off Clew Bay. He told he was either going to murder him or leave him stranded there unless he dropped all the charges. His father, not surprisingly acquiesced, but Fitzgerald continued his wicked ways and it didn't surprise many people when he was hanged on the gallows at the age of 38 after murdering one of his many enemies.

Fitzpatrick, Pat
When this journalist rang a restaurant to ask if they had wheelchair access he was informed they accepted all major credit cards.

Suggests a new shampoo for bald men: Shoulders.

Flanagan, Oliver J (1920-87)
Said there was no sex in Ireland before The Late Late Show. Which makes one wonder where he came from.

Flanagan, Willie (1867-1925)
An eccentric who rarely went anywhere without his horse – including the theatre. Once interrupted a play by riding it across the stage. Another time he rode it into the bar counter of the Gresham Hotel and demanded that it be given a drink. He was only four feet tall and needed a ladder to get on to it.

Flanagan was also a practical joker of some note. He arrived at the Olympia Theatre one night during World War I dressed as The Kaiser. Another time, after failing to win a fancy dress competition where he went as a bird, he went up to the judge's table in protest and 'laid an egg'. Afterwards he became 'The Bird' Flanagan.

Ford, John (1895-1973)
When a producer told him he was three days behind on a film shoot once, tore up the script and said to the producer, 'Now I'm three days *ahead.*'

Had a love-hate relationship with Maureen O'Hara, being infatuated with her but treating her terribly on all the films he made with her. One day he drew a selection of penises on a piece of paper in front of her to intimidate her. Another day he broke into her house and stole her record collection. Tried to get her brother Jimmy arrested in Mexico on a bogus drugs charge.

Made five films with her and was yet heard to say, 'She couldn't act her way out of a brick shithouse.'

Won three Oscars but didn't turn up at either ceremony. The first time he went fishing, for the second he was at ward and for the third drunk.

Asked by Peter Bogdanovich how he liked to shoot Monument Valley, he replied, 'With a camera.'

Fowlie, R.S.J.
This enterprising Constable, who was attached to the Canal Street Barracks in Newry, fought off twenty female rivals to win a 'Beautiful Ankle' competition at a fancy dress event held in 1927. The faces of the competitors were hidden behind a screen, making the deception fairly easy.

French, Katy (1983-2007)
Said she was so vain she even smiled at speed cameras.

French, Percy (1850-1920)
French often criticised the West Clare train which travelled between Ennis and Kilkee in the early years of the last century. One driver, he averred, was given to stopping the train in the middle of nowhere and then wandering across a field on mysterious errands. Another driver was renowned for backing the train into the station it had just departed to pick up latecomers – and then providing them with hot water bottles to keep their feet warm in winter.

Another day the train pulled up suddenly in the middle of the countryside. When a passenger asked what was wrong, the driver said, 'There's a cow on the line.' It was removed and he drove off again at snail's pace. Half an hour later the train stopped again. The driver got out and the passenger said, 'Is there another cow on the line? The drive replied, 'No, it's the same one!'

French was sued for libel after writing a song that said the train was frequently unpunctual. On the day he was due to appear in court he was late. When the judge asked him why he replied, 'Because I was on the West Clare Railway, Your Honour.'

Fricker, Brendan (1944-)
Won an Oscar for My Left Foot. Afterwards she said she was going to buy a new house. Why? Because she wanted to put in on a mantel-piece and the house she had didn't have one.

Friel, Brian (1929-2015)
Confessed to having had 'an exhausting affair' with his school teacher Ms Crossley before he was ten. He tried to impress her by cycling backwards outside her house on his new bicycle, his bottom resting precariously on the

handlebars as he careered madly up and down the road. Sadly, she wasn't seduced by this apparition. He fell off eventually and had to go to the hospital for a month. She didn't even visit him. All he had to show for his passion was 'two over-developed muscles on the back of my legs.'

Gale, Sean
Tipperary man who was arrested in Clonmel in 1995 for driving with a pair of pliers instead of a steering wheel. 'It came off when I was visiting the mother-in-law,' he explained to police.

Gallagher PJ (1975-)
A woman threw her knickers at him one night during his comedy act. After he was finished she asked for them back. 'Normally I wouldn't need them,' she said, 'but they're part of a set.'

Is adopted. Because most of the people he knew in childhood were also adopted, grew up believing the children who weren't adopted were the odd ones.

Gallagher, Victoria
Believes more people have read Harry Potter than are alive.

Gallen, Conal
Refuses to travel on Virgin Airlines because he doesn't like planes that don't go all the way.

Always sit on the back seats of planes because he never heard of one reversing into a mountain.

Began to get worried his wife might be having an affair when he moved from Dublin to Donegal and found he had the same milkman.

Galway, James (1934-)
Was once offered a 'bread sandwich' on a plane journey. It consisted of two slices of bread... and another one in the middle.

Hates the description of himself as a flautist. 'I have never played a flaut,' he assures us.

Garson, Greer (1904-96)
Won an Oscar for playing the title character in the 1942 war drama Mrs Miniver. During the making of it she was sleeping with Richard Ney, who played her son in the film. She married him the following year.

Went on so long in her Oscar speech, a rule was applied afterwards limiting the time all winners were allowed. One person in attendance at the ceremonies said, 'The speech seemed to last longer than the war.'

Geldof, Bob (1954-)
People keep telling him you get grumpier as you get older. 'That would be difficult for me,' he admits.

Once went to the pictures every day for three months.

George, Boy (1961-)
Had a childhood ambition to be like Shirley Bassey.

Describes himself as the 'pink sheep' of his family.

Says he'd like to be reincarnated as Matt Dillon's underwear.

Prefers tea to sex.

Giles, Johnny (1940-)
Once said, I'd rather play in front of a full stadium than an empty crowd.'

Believed Jack Charlton wasn't always right but he was never wrong.

Gill, Vincent (1909-76)
Gill was the founder of the Longford News. He had an unusual way of getting people to take out subscriptions to the paper. He would frequently interrupt courting couples in compromising positions and tell them if they didn't take out a 'sub', he'd publish their names the following week. If they threatened to sue him, he'd tell them he had no money so there'd be no point. He often ended up in the canal at Longford as a result of some of the articles he wrote but he never bored anyone.

Gill liked to drink, which cut into his writing time. One week he was short of feature material so printed a full page in black, giving it the caption: 'Black-out in Drumlish.'

Ginnity Noel V.
Knew an atheist who married a Jehovah's Witness. 'Now they have children who knock at your door for no apparent reason.'

Wonders why, when the doorbell rings, the dog thinks it's always for him.

Says he spent some time as a podiatrist to Dolly Parton but gave up because he didn't like working in the dark.

Bought a non-stick frying pan but couldn't get the label off.

Is old enough to remember Elvis 'when he was alive the first time.'

Gave back a tie he bought one because it was too tight.

Says he so short he's the only person in Ireland whose feet are in his passport photograph.

Gogan, Larry
The veteran DJ says his age is a state secret. Declan Lynch puts his age at 'approximately 40,000 years.'

Has got some howlers of answers to his 'Just-a-Minute Quiz' over the years. Perhaps the most memorable when he asked a contestant to complete the phrase, 'As happy as...' He gave a hint: 'Think of me.' The contestant said, 'A pig in shite.'

Gogarty, Oliver St. John (1878-1957)
Said to a friend one sunny day, 'It is most extraordinary weather for this time of year.' The friend replied, 'Ah, it isn't this time of year at all.'

Hated the rosary growing up so much he used to put whiskey in his cat's milk to create a distraction during the saying of it.

Was captured by republicans during the Civil War. Was about to be shot by the banks of the Liffey. Asked if he could 'relieve nature.' His request granted he shook himself free of his captors and dived into the freezing river – it was December – and swam to the other side amidst a hail of bullets. In honour of his miraculous survival he donated two swans to the Liffey afterwards.

Described Finnegans Wake as Joyce talking in his sleep.

Goldsmith, Oliver (1728-74)
When he was at college he was discovered one morning by a fellow student in bed covered with feathers. Asked to explain what happened he told the student he'd met a woman the previous evening who was so poor he gave her all his clothes and also the blankets from his bed. He woke up freezing in the middle of the night and cut his mattress open with a knife to get the feathers out so he could warm himself.

Gorman, Michael John
Director of Dublin Science Gallery in 2009. Said shaking hands at religious ceremonies carried the risk of swine flu. A kiss was safer, he advised, because hands carried more bacteria.

Grace, Brendan (1951-2019)
Said he got a packet of batteries one Christmas 'and they weren't included.'

Described himself as being 'under-tall' rather than 'overweight.' The correct height for his weight, he makes out, is approximately seven feet ten and a half inches.

Didn't believe in going to bed mad. Because of this, his wife and himself once stayed up six months after an argument.

Said his wife closes her eyes when he makes love to her – because she hates to see him enjoying himself.

Bought an electric chair for his mother-in-law one Christmas but she refused to plug it in.

Said he would have preferred to be dead than buried in a Protestant graveyard.

Grady, Patrick (1700-96)
Was born on the same day as his twin sister Eleanor, July 27, 1700. They were also married on the same day and died on the same day 96 years later, leaving the same number of descendants.

Lady Gregory (1852-1932)
When she was asked what was the meaning of the Celtic Revival she said, 'It's a movement to persuade the Scots to buy our books while we continue not to buy theirs.'

Guiney, Michael
Once put this sign on his shop window: 'Closed on Account of Re-Opening.'

Hall, Frank (1921-95)
Hall was a film censor for a time. He said once, 'Sometimes the certificate given to a film depends on the censor's piles while he's watching it.'

Believed the best way to lie about your age was the opposite to most people: 'If you're 39, tell them you're 55. They'll say, 'You look brilliant.'

Hamilton W. J.
Lighthouse keeper from Skellig, off the Kerry coast, who made false teeth for himself in the 1930s from the ivory handles of knives.

Hamilton, William Rowan (1805-65)
Hamilton was a physicist, a mathematician and a scientist. He was also a child prodigy, and able to converse in nine

different languages by the age of seven. A few years later he doubled that number of tongues.

Became so engrossed in his speculations he often forgot to eat.

Hamilton, George (1951-)
This football commentator has occasionally been afflicted with 'foot-in-mouth disease.' On one occasion during a match he expounded, 'He caught that with the outside of his instep.' On another occasion he was heard to say, 'The Baggio brothers, of course, are not related.'

Another of his pronouncements was, 'Welcome to the Nou Camp Stadium in Barcelona, which is packed to capacity with some patches of seats left empty.'

Said at a later match, 'There's no telling what the score will be if this one goes in.'

Harris, Richard (1932-2002)
Was confined to bed for three years with TB as a young man. Used to spend a lot of time looking up at the ceiling. Eventually invented people to talk to from the light bulbs, casting himself as a king or a Pope talking to them.

Loved having affairs with women but got bored with them soon after. Told them they weren't allowed to speak to him, just nod their heads. Got rid of them by pretending he had ghosts in his house.

Was dyslexic. Came back to the Beverly Hills Hotel one night drunk and there was nobody behind the desk. Picked up key 23 instead of key 32. When he got to the room he took off all his clothes and lay on the bed. Suddenly the light went on and he realised he was lying between a naked man and woman. They were on their honeymoon. They said, 'You're Richard Harris, aren't you?' They didn't kick him out. Instead they brought him down to the wedding breakfast the next morning. Then they had some Bloody Marys together.

Was so drunk once he proposed marriage to a man. 'He should have accepted,' Harris said, 'I pay good alimony.'

Drank so much in his life, felt he should have been in the Record Book of Guinnesses.

Didn't see himself as an eco warrior: 'My idea of recycling is to use a beer can as an ashtray.'

Hated Charlton Heston's obsession with time when he made Major Dundee with him. Arrived on the set one day with a huge collection of alarm clocks, including one tied around his neck. He set them so they would all go off at the exact same time. When Heston heard the din he jumped in the air in shock. Said Harris, 'Relax, it's just me 'clocking' in early for once.'

Asked what was the difference between himself and Tom Cruise he said, 'Tom goes to film premieres with a bottle of Evian water. I used to carry wine.' Landed himself in jail and/or hospital many times after binges. Once time, mad for drink, he threw stones up at the window of a house he happened to be passing. The woman inside took pity on him and he ended up staying with her for four days.

In 1948 he led the workforce of his father's flour business into a strike for higher pay! His father never forgave him. The resulting unrest ultimately led to the mill closing down.

For Harris Junior, the absurdity of the situation had a wonderful logic to it.

Said he could never write his autobiography because he was too drunk to remember most of what happened to him.

During the shooting of 'Mutiny on the Bounty' had a row with Marlon Brando that resulted in him refusing to act beside him, playing most of his scenes to a little green box upon which he drew Brando's features.

Asked what he felt was necessary to be a good actor he replied, 'A cannibalistic quality.'

Was so anxious to get the lead role in 'Camelot' he dressed up as a waiter at a cocktail party one night and stood in front of the movie's director, Joshua Logan, whom he'd known was going to be at it. Logan, fed up with being pestered by him, shouted out, 'Will you leave me alone for Christ's sake?' Harris stood firm and replied, 'Never. Wherever you go, I'll be there. If you go to the toilet, I'll pop out of the bowl. If you catch a taxi, I'll jump in beside you. If you're on a plane, I'll be in the next seat.' Logan eventually gave in and handed him the part.

Once wrote a novel, 'Flanney', about a man who refuses to be born.

When he was married to Elizabeth, his first wife, he went out to get the papers one night... and returned ten days later. Instead of buying the papers he flew to Shannon Airport and went on the tear with some friends from Limerick. Knowing he'd be in the doghouse with her when he came back, he hired a sandwich man to stand outside his door carrying a board that said, 'In the name of Jesus, love thy neighbour

Harris.' When his wife answered the door he said to her, 'Why didn't you pay the ransom?' After which she hit him with a rolling pin.

Once spent eight hours arguing with Jim Sheridan, the director of the movie 'The Field', in which he played the character of the Bull McCabe, over whether the word 'mother' should be changed to 'widow' for one of his lines of dialogue.

Had an ambition to die at 110 writing poetry, sipping Guinness and serenading a woman.

Was given the Last Rites five times before he was fifty. One time as the priest prepared to hear his confession, Harris said, 'If I go into detail about my sexual escapades, you'll mourn the day you took a vow of celibacy.' (The priest, perhaps wisely, opted to hear a 'general' confession instead before giving him absolution).

Harrison, Gerry
This Ballyshannon man was driving near his home one night when he was stopped by guards. Seeing no tax disc on display, they asked him to produce it. As he did so he proceeded to eat it. When they asked him why he did this he said, 'Because I was hungry.' He later said he hadn't eaten the disc at all but rather an air freshener cover which he felt constrained to dispose of because it featured a photo of a scantily-clad woman.

Haughey, Charles (1925-2006)
To get a vote, said Hugh Leonard, the former Taoiseach would have roller-skated backwards into a nunnery, naked from the waist down and singing 'Kevin Barry' in Swahili.

When a widow asked him for advice on how she could improve her financial circumstances in the tough economic climate he said, 'Get married again.'

He roared so much at a junior TD one day, the man became confused and couldn't find the door out of the office. He asked Haughey for assistance only to be told, 'Why don't you jump out the fucking window?'

Coined the term GUBU ('Grotesque, unbelievable, bizarre, unprecedented' to the events of 1982 when Malcolm Arthur went on a killing spree. Some people felt the acronym might also have been an apt description of Haughey's own career. Conor Cruise O'Brien said, 'If I saw Mr Haughey buried at midnight with a stake driven through this heart, I would continue to wear a glove of garlic around my neck just in case.'

Healy-Rae, Jackie (1931-2014)
The controversial politician also owned a pub in Kerry. It had a condom machine in the toilet. He met a farmer in there one day who was scrutinising it carefully. 'Why in the name of God,' he said to him, 'do you keep the cigarette dispenser in the jacks?'

Herbert, Dorothea
In her book *Retrospections*, published in 1781, Herbert tells the story of a Mrs Cooke from Clontarf who was so distraught over her husband's death that she ordered her whole house to be painted black and the outhouses as well, including the stable doors and hay mangers. Even flowerpots had to be blackened. An upholsterer was also employed to make black beds, black chair covers and black curtains. When he heard he was to be locked in a room until he agreed to all this he made a break for freedom.

Healy, Maurice
Had a teacher who could, as he put it, 'spit in nine languages.'

Healy, Shay (1943-)
Asked how many times he looked in a mirror per day he replied, '247. No, wait – 248.'

Higgins, Alex (1949-2010)
Won his first world championship in 1972 but gambled the money away. Was virtually homeless at this time. Lived in a row of abandoned houses in Blackburn which were awaiting demolition. Each time one was pulled down he moved to the house next door to it until he eventually ran out of houses.

Won the Benson & Hedges Irish Masters on crutches one year.

'He could pick a fight with a lamp-post,' said his friend Jimmy White. White told a story of one night when Higgins lost his temper and tried to throw a TV set out a window, not realising it was closed at the time. The television bounced off the window and back into his arms.

Listed his idols as George Best, Muhammad Ali, John McEnroe and God. In that order.

Was fined £1500 for peeing into a potted plant in the 1980s. 'I often wonder how it's doing,' he said later. 'Maybe it's learned to screw back.'

The best exercise he got towards the end of his life, he said, was coughing.

Higgins, Maeve (1981-)
She was born, she says, with a thick black mop of curly hair, and a pair of high heels.

Her least appealing traits are: Getting xenophobic when she's jet-lagged, thinking about how fat Americans are, and what terrible soldiers Italians make.

When she dies, she'd like to have her ashes scattered from the top of the power station in Aghada onto a tray of freshly baked raspberry scones.

Higgins, Rita Ann (1955-)
Revealed some years ago that Pope John 23rd was actually a member of her family, his full name being Pope John 23rd Higgins.

Thinks people who wear cardigans are subversive.

Hinkson, Katherine Tynan (1861-1931)
This lady isn't quite a household name in Ireland despite writing over a hundred novels, 18 books of poetry and 12 collections of short stories and five volumes of autobiography.

Hodgers, Jennifer (1843-1915)
Louth woman who pretended she was a man so she could fight in the American Civil War. She enlisted in the Union Army as Albert Cashier and fought in over forty battles. After the war she worked as a janitor, a gravedigger and a streetlighter. She got a pension after she retired but was knocked down by a car in 1911 and taken to hospital with a broken leg. Here her true identity was discovered. An investigation followed. When it was established that she'd genuinely fought in the said battles, the pension was

maintained by Hodgers developed dementia and was moved to a hospital for the insane in 1913. She died two years later and was buried with full military honours.

Hook, George (1941-)
Says stacking the dishwasher represents his sole contribution to domesticity.

Horan, Fr Cornelius (1947-)
Kerry-born (laicised) priest who ran onto the track of the British Grand Prix in 2003 wearing a kilt and waving a banner that said, 'Read The Bible. The Bible is Always Right.' He was arrested for aggravated trespass and sentenced to two months in jail but the following summer he was up to his tricks again, interrupting the marathon race at the Athens Olympics by running on to the track in a floppy green tam-o-shanter and commencing to do a soft jig. He pushed the race leader off the track in his excitement and ruined his chances of a gold medal.

He was arrested for assaulting a seven year old girl in 2004 but found not guilty. That year also he was wrestled to the ground by police at the Epsom derby because they suspected he intended to run out in front of the horses and stop the race. He interrupted the Wimbledon tennis championships and the World Cup in subsequent years, and told people he intended to carry posters declaring the fact that Hitler was a good leader who followed the word of Christ. During the war in Iraq he wrote to Saddam Hussein offering to do a jig in front of his family.

Fr Horan is also a writer, having published an ebook, 'A Glorious New World Very Soon to Come', predicting the end of the world, and an electronic booklet entitled 'Christ Will Soon Take Power From All the Governments.' It predicts the fact that Jesus will rule the world from Jerusalem in the future, and that there will be basically two classes of people in the world at that point: 'Immortal saints' who'll rule for a millennium and 'Mortal Citizens' who will become Jewish and rule for (only) 900 years.

When Prince William had his first child, Fr Horan attended the occasion with placards saying 'Queen Elizabeth Was Probably Foretold in the Bible' and 'I am Neil Horan. I Perform at Weddings. My Mission In Life Is To Prepare The World For The Second Coming.'

Horgan, Shane
Joined the hordes of people looking for a refund from the ill-fated Barbara Streisand concert in Dublin in 2007. His reasons, however, were different to those of other people: 'I could actually hear her singing.'

Houlihan, Con (1925-2012)
The much-loved journalist said he liked to 'watch' football games on the radio.

When he was a young boy at school, a priest asked him what he wanted to be when he grew up. 'A bandit,' he replied.

Thought you could hear hens dreaming if you eavesdropped on them. One time when he was in Spain he claimed he had an extraordinary moment of communication with one of them.

Said he didn't marry because he never found a woman who could understand apostrophes and 'You can never trust a woman who misuses the apostrophe.'

Missed Italia '90, he said, because he was at it. The people who stayed at home saw much more of it than we did.'

Used to put milk in his brandy.

Saw a sign when he was in Mexico that said, 'When there are earthquakes, please use the stairs.'

Hourihane, Ann-Marie
Says her favourite form of relaxation is wondering what happened to the Number 10 bus.

Howard, Paul (1971-)
Believes Bram Stoker was inspired to write about a bloodsucking vampire from his previous experience in a South Dublin estate agency.

Describes the 46A bus as a vehicle that eventually reaches Monkstown after a circuitous path that also takes in Ayers Rock, Angkor Wat and Puerto Mereno glacier.

Amy Huberman (1979-)
Says she's not a full Jew, just Jew-ish.

Hughes, Sean (1966-2017)
Once claimed his father lost his hair overnight. In a poker game.

Was flattered to be asked to write 700 words for The Guardian as it gave him the opportunity to use his entire vocabulary. Twice.

Thanked God for 'messing up my life and also not existing, which is quite an achievement.'

Said he's never paid for sex in his life. 'Which has really pissed off some of the prostitutes I've been with.'

Went to a Muslim speed-dating evening one night. The expression he heard most often was, 'Nice eyes.'

Claimed to have been disappointed at the acquittal of O.J. Simpson because 'I was squatting in his house at the time and I had to move out when he came home.'

Won a pair of sneakers off Kurt Cobain when they were playing Russian Roulette together one night.

Said he first became aware of the great intelligence of dolphins when he was swimming with a group of them one time and they kept ganging up on him and dunking his head under the water.

Insisted his school life wasn't normal: 'Other boys in my class smoked behind the bicycle shed. I cycled around behind the tobacconist's shop.'

Thought he got his rebellious streak from his father: 'He used to abuse people and then ask them for money. But then he left the priesthood.'

Got so drunk one night he thought he was in a karaoke bar when he was just sitting at home watching a film on TV with subtitles.

Hunniford, Gloria (1940-)
When Roger Bannister broke the four-minute mile record, thought it would now only take her eight minutes to walk to her school, which was two miles away.

Once saw a sign on a window in Belfast: 'Buy Now While Shops Last.'

When she was dating she thought she could get pregnant after courting sessions even if she was wearing knickers.

Believes the secret of doing the waltz perfectly is to dance 'as if your partner has B.O.'

Went to the toilet in Buckingham Palace 'because I wanted to leave something behind.'

Huston, John (1906-87)
Asked why he cast a real-life princess as a peasant in his film 'A Walk with Love and Death', replied, 'I couldn't find anyone who looked more like a peasant.'

Ingoldsby, Pat (1942-)
Ireland's loopiest writer used to go around the place with phones on his head talking to trees. He's now toned it down a bit and lives relatively quietly with his cats when he's not selling his books in Dublin's city centre.

Once offered a 'mobile phone euthanasia' serviced to distressed phone users who wished to dispense with their devices.

Wrote a poem called 'Vagina in the Vatican' about a vagina that managed to avoid security in that building because nobody knew what it was – or at least pretended not to.

Has his poems protected from inclusion in anything that has the word 'Arts' in it by dint of something he refers to as The Bratislava Accord, 1993, Section 2.

Proposed a solution to Dublin's handbag-snatching problem by the introduction of 'talking handbags' which would be electronically programmed to respond to the owner's touch and would whisper reassuringly to the tip of a familiar finger, 'Don't worry about a thing. I know it's you.' A strange hand, on the other, er, hand, would hear the opening chords of 'The 1812 Overture' and a voice would bark out, 'Hark and Hist, Get They Thieving Hands Off Me, Thou Nefarious Brigand.'

Likes open plan shops with no counters: 'Many shop assistants are only used to dealing with the top halves of people. They only ever see us from the waist up. For this reason a lot of them have developed an unreasoning fear of people's bottom halves.

Knew a woman who thought her bedroom radiator was trying to seduce her because it only made noises when her husband went to the toilet.

Often wonders what the man who discovered cows could give milk was up to at the time of his discovery.

Once printed a poem written on his computer by his cat. The cat holds the copyright.

Bought a record one time that wouldn't play properly. He took it back to the shop and the proprietor put it on his hi-fi, where it played perfectly. As a result, he refused to exchange it. Ingoldsby wasn't impressed. 'The next time I feel like playing it,' he said, ' I'll come back here with all my friends and we can have a few pints and sit around listening to it.'

Went into a video shop once to rent out a film. The woman behind the counter loved his writing and they had a chat about it. He then put the film he wanted on the counter. 'Have you got ID?' she asked him. 'You know who I am,' he said. 'I know,' she said, 'but I can't give you the film without you verifying your identity.'

Can never remember people's names. Thinks it would be a good idea if we all had them tattooed onto our foreheads.

After he reached fifty, rang up Aras an Urachtarain and discovered he'd received a cheque for £250 when he got to a hundred. 'That's great,' he said, 'but could you let me have half the money upfront?'

Doesn't know why so many seagulls practice their 'bombing raids' on Daniel O'Connell's statue in Dublin's city centre but leave all the other ones alone. Is it that they've never heard of Catholic Emancipation?

Pat has revealed that his first sexual experience took place at a bus stop. 'I slid down and thought, 'That's lovely' so I did it again. I was into bus stops for months after that.' Ingoldsby confided: 'I had a crush on one particular one outside the library. It was the most sexually fulfilling bus stop in Malahide.'

His story has a sad ending, however, because after such experiences, he found it hard to relate to the gentle sex. The reason? 'You can't slide down a woman.'

Jacob, Joshua (1805-77)
Founder of the White Quakers, a sect whose members always dressed in white, destroyed anything ornamental in their houses, avoided luxuries like meat in their diet, and embraced simple living. Such simplicity described the wearing of gaudy clothing, which no doubt promoted Joshua

to organise a nude march through Dublin in the course of which the Quakers smashed up anything they saw that they didn't like.

Was prone to visions, most notably one of a wild elephant he did his best to fight with a rope on a quay at Clonmel.

Jimeoin (1966-)
Doesn't believe rainbows are optical illusions: 'They only look like them.'

Once had a psychic girlfriend but she left him before they met.

Believes two out of every one person in Ireland is schizoid.

Jordan, Neil (1951-)
Asked once what was the worst aspect of being a film-maker in Ireland, he replied, 'There are no direct flights to L.A.'

Finds it difficult working with actors who want to know details of a character's past. 'I always say they're out-of-work saxophone players,' he says.

Has an ambition to write a book about Hollywood called 'Seven Ways to Avoid Decapitation.'

According to 'In Dublin' magazine, he once used the expression 'Y'know' 125 times in a 25-minute interview.

Spent some time as a young man doing street theatre in St. Stephen's Green dressed up as a fish in a skintight leotard.

Joyce, James (1882-1941)
When a portrait painter said he wanted to capture his soul, Joyce said, 'Don't worry about my soul. Just get my tie right.'

Described women as creatures who micturated once a day, defecated once a week, menstruated once a month and parturiated once a year. Said the best way to find out if a woman was a good bet was to bring her to an art gallery. 'If she breaks wind, she's all right', he advised.

His attention to detail in Ulysses was such that he claimed Dublin could be re-built from its pages if it was ever bombed. In 1921 he wrote to his aunt Josephine from Trieste and asked, 'Is it possible for an ordinary person to climb over the railings of No. 7 Eccles Street' – where Leopold Bloom lived – 'and lower himself from them till his feet are within two or three feet of the ground and drop unhurt? I require this information in order to determine the wording of a paragraph.'

Engaged in sado-masochistic games with his wife Nora, writing a letter to her once that said, 'I wish you would smack me flog me even. Not in play, dear, but in earnest, and on my naked flesh. I wish you would smack me or flog me even. Not in play, dear, but in earnest, and on my naked flesh. I wish you were strong and had a big full proud bosom and big fat thighs. I would love to be whipped by you, Nora love.'

Wanted Nora to put on weight so she could and tease him more effectively. Had a fetish for her soiled underwear. Fantasised about her having affairs. Encouraged her to have one so he could use it to get inspiration for his work.

Met Marcel Proust at a literary dinner one night. Everybody was wondering what pearls of wisdom they might exchange about books but the chemistry wasn't great between them. Proust said to Joyce, 'Do you like truffles?' Joyce replied, 'I am very fond of them.' Soon afterwards, the pair went their separate ways.

When he was writing Ulysses his friend Frank Budgen asked him how it was going. 'I worked hard on it all day today,' Joyce told him.' Does that mean you've written a great deal?' asked Budgeon. 'Two sentences,' Joyce replied.

Saw himself as 'An Irish teetotaller', by which he meant he didn't take alcohol between drinks.

Believed the British beatitudes were 'Beer, beef, business, Bibles, bulldogs, battleships, buggery and bishops.'

Was terrified of thunder. Used to hide in closets to avoid it. Also feared dogs.

Carried rings and rabbits' ears around with him to ward off evil spirits. Thought an empty bottle on a table brought bad luck.

Was an underwear fetishist. Kept a pair of doll's panties with him at all times. Used to put them on his fingers and 'walk' them across bar counters.

Wrote Finnegans Wake to keep academics in meaningless theses until they were carted out of universities in pine boxes. The only demand he made of his readers, he claimed, was that they devote their whole lives to wading through his books.

Kavanagh, Liz
Thinks her grandchildren are so wonderful she's sorry she didn't have them first.

Kavanagh, Paddy (1904-67)
Was in McDaid's pub one night reading the work of a poet he didn't like. When the barman came over with his drink he spilled it over the book. Kavanagh said to him, 'You might never make a barman, son, but you're a fuckin' good judge of poetry.

Was know as 'The Canal Bank Pote' because of his fondness for the Baggot Street Canal. Was walking beside it one night muttering to himself, as he was wont to do, 'Lord commemorate me where there's water,' he said. At this point an enemy of his strode up behind him. 'I'll give you water, you fuckin made poet,' he said, and pushed him into the canal. Kavanagh thought he was going to drown but fought hard and got himself out. Some years later, the two men became friends. The man who pushed him said he was consumed with remorse and asked for his forgiveness. Kavanagh gave it. Shortly afterwards, the man's wife gave birth to a slightly handicapped child. He thought this was God punishing him for what he did to Kavanagh. He asked Kavanagh to come around to his house and try and heal the child by the laying on of hands. 'You won't have seen the like of it in the Abbey,' said Kavanagh.

Keane, John B. (1928-2002)
When he played football as a young man he got this advice from a friend: 'Keep your high balls low.'

Was given out to by a man in a bar in Killarney once for never having written about bucket handles.

Thought Irish people could never be happy 'until everyone has had more than everyone else.'

Believed the most important literary awards should go to a writer called Anon.

Regarded the propagation of bingo as the ultimate role of the Catholic Church in Ireland.

Keely, Terence (? – 1953)
Keely was a Dubliner who spent most of his life telling people he would become president of Ireland one day. If he was elected, he said the first thing he would do would be to turn Nelson's Pillar back to front so Daniel O'Connell wouldn't have to look into the face of The Auld Enemy. Used to appear in Lord Edward Street pushing a handcart on the days of presidential inaugurations, the name KEELY proudly displayed on his (silk) top hat.

Keenan, Brian (1950-)
Was bundled into the boot of a car by kidnappers in Belfast in 1986. Spent four years in captivity in Beirut afterwards. When asked why he never tried to escape, he said, 'It would have been difficult trying to avoid detection walking around Beirut in my underpants.'

Ordered a taxi from Dublin Airport one day soon afterwards. After he sat in, the driver said to him, 'Are you sure you wouldn't be ;more comfortable in the boot?'

At his first press conference he said, 'I'm going to visit all the countries in the world, eat all the food in the world, drink all the drink in the world and make love to all the women in the world.'

Instead of that he just wrote some books.

Kelly, David (1929-2012)
Lost so many years of his life through drink, it was 1970 before he learned John F. Kennedy had been assassinated.

Kelly, Eamonn (1914-2001)
The famous story-teller knew an 85-year-old man who married a girl of 18. He wanted someone to answer the rosary for him.

Believed there were just two seasons in Ireland: June and winter.

Kelly, Ned (1854-80)
The famous Australia-Irish bandit was so ashamed of his baldness he rode around with a bucket on his head.

Kelly, Owen
Knew a man who refused to leave his house after he got sick. Thought there was something 'splendidly Irish' about staying away from the doctor because of illness.

Once saw a reference written by a man for a job applicant he didn't like. It went, 'I've known this gentleman for twenty years. He does not smoke.'

Kelly, Sorcha
Wrote about a court case where a man stole 757 sweaters, 733 shirts, 460 dresses, 403 jackets, 83 pairs of socks and 286 pairs of children's trousers. His defence was that he had a large family.

Kenny, Jim (1936-97)
Defined an Irish exorcism as 'trying to get the priest out of your son.'

Kennedy, Maria Doyle (1964-)
Believes the greatest cultural annoyance in Ireland today is supermarket trolleys that won't go straight.

Kennelly, Brendan
A woman greeted him once with the words, 'I believe you've just turned 75. You don't look a day over 74.'

Kenny, Jon (1957-)
Says he's not known outside Ireland but in Waterford he's world famous.

Knew a woman once who was so thin, 'the one eye would have done her.'

Kerr, Brian (1953-)
When Kerr was managing Ireland's Under 18s they beat a UN squad 22-nil in a match in Cyprus in 1998. The gloss was taken off the victory, Kerr felt, by the fact that the 21st goal was offside.

Saint Kevin (498-618)
This 6th century hermit lived in a cave in Wicklow. He spent half his time praying and the other half, if we're to believe the legend, fending off the advances of a woman called Kathleen who tried to wean him away from the path of righteousness. He punished himself by stripping naked and lying down in a bed of nettles, but when Kathleen discovered his hiding place he used the nettles on her instead. Eventually decided she was the devil and pushed

her into a nearby lake. Afterwards he befriended a mouse, deciding they were more dependable than women.

Keyes, Marian (1963-)
Fell in love for the first time at fifteen: with a pair of four-inch black patent platform wedges with an ankle strap.

Admits she'd 'dither' if she was offered a choice between world peace and a Prada handbag. Is not proud of this.

Doesn't like her face in photos. Thinks it looks like something Picasso painted during his Cubist period.

Says she suffers from 'shopping bulimia'. Is always getting stuff and then trying to give it back.

Claims biting her fingernails is the only exercise she gets.

Feels Irishmen resolutely refuse to go to the doctor. Even if their leg falls off they'll say, 'I'm grand. I never really used it much anyway.'

Generally tried to better herself but thinks she's fighting a losing battle. One year she made a New Year Resolution not to make a New Year Resolution.

Kiely, Benedict (1919-2007)
Once day when the writer walked from O'Connell Street to the White Horse Bar, a distance of less than 75 yards, fourteen different people invited him to have a drink with them.

Said a Tyrone woman would never buy a rabbit without a head in case it turned out to be a cat.

Kilduff, Paul
Thinks the easiest job in the world must be a weather forecaster in Southern Spain: 'Tomorrow it's going to be hot.'

Saint Killian
The only Irishman ever offered the job of Pope. The wise man declined.

Kirwan, Richard (1733-1812)
This sometime president of the Irish Academy had such a fear of flies that he paid his servants a sizeable reward for any they killed and presented to him. He always wore a hat whether he was indoors or outdoors and also liked to walk around with his pet eagle perched on his shoulder.

Knuttel, Graham (1954-2023)
Failed all his exams at school so he'd be sent to art school instead.

Fortunately this wasn't difficult.

Legge, Thomas (? – 1808)
This adventurous soul left his native Donaghadee, County Down to become a mercenary in India but things didn't work out for him and he was soon on the streets begging. He then turned his attention to trying to heal people, using sheep's bones to affect cures. Afterwards the versatile man was put in charge of an army, but he showed as little facility for this as he did for healing or making money. He was injured severely in his first battle and failed to heal himself, even with sheep's bones. Ended his days as a fakir living naked in a desert tomb outside Jaipur.

Lillis, Lorraine
UCD researcher who advised farmers to give their cattle fish oil to cut down on the level of cow farts in 2009. 'The oil affects the methane-producing bacteria in the rumen part of the cow's gut,' she explained, 'leading to reduced emissions.' The cows couldn't be reached for comment.

Linehan, Rosaleen (1937-)
Believes that Irish children today don't live at home until *after* they're married.

Looney, Fiona
To date, the busy journalist/playwright/novelist/mother reckons she's put '9855' nappes on her children's bottoms.

Has a friend who consoled herself over her marriage break-up by buying a small reading lamp in Ikea.

Lynch, Brid (1898-1964)
Cork woman whose husband passed away in the early 1900s. When she was asked how it happened she replied, 'He died in his sleep and doesn't know he's dead yet. If he woke up the shock would probably kill him.'

Lynch, Joe (1925-2001)
The actor loved Cork hurlers so much, he said, that if he found one of them in bed with his wife he'd go downstairs and make him a cup of tea.

Lynch, Katherine
Wouldn't consider having a child after thirty: '29 of the little buggers is enough.'

Said Louis Walsh clapped like someone trying to catch a fart.

Would like to rule Ireland so she could turn Roscommon into a handball alley.

Believes men were only invented because vibrators can't mow the lawn.

Lynd, Robert (1879-1949)
Knew a man who had a paranoid belief that detectives were following him wherever he went. Spent half his life, Lynd said, stopping at lamp-posts to tie his shoelaces so he could let them pass.

MacArthur, Malcolm (1945-)
After brutally killing a nurse in the Phoenix Park in 1982 he managed to get an ambulance escort to a hospital afterwards with her body. Two days later, after another murder, he went to the All-Ireland hurling semi-final in Croke Park, sitting in the VIP box. Rounded the day off with a trip back to the house of Ireland's Attorney General, where he was staying. As you would.

MacBride, Maud Gonne (1988-1953)
'Celebrated' the Golden Jubilee of Queen Victoria in 1897 by draping a coffin with a black cloth and parading it around Dublin.

Was cruelly dubbed 'Gond Mad' instead of 'Maud Gonne' in old age as she developed what Michael Mac Liammoir called 'grand romantic dottiness.'

MacGowan, Shane (1957-)
At school, he confessed, he was 'Minister for Torture': 'I put dustbin lids over kids' heads and banged them for half and hour. I got stinging nettles and rubbed their balls with them,

tweaked their nipples and generally abused them. That was before I read the Marquis de Sade. Sadism is a fairly normal condition.

At the sleeve of a Beach Boys album one time in protest at its blandness.

Believes Samuel Beckett's depression could be traced back to the fact that he wanted to play cricket for Ireland but they didn't have a team.

MacGowran, Jack
Once said to a judge in a courtroom after an offence, 'I was sober enough to know I was drunk.'

MacHale, Des (1946-)
Says you can always tell a Kerryman on an oil rig. He's the one throwing breadcrumbs at the helicopters.

Has seen the movie The Quiet Man over 200 times.

Mac Liammoir, Michael (1899-1978)
Liked his toupee so much he even refused to take it off when playing a bald man in the TV series Tolka Row in the 1960s. Instead he put a bald headpiece over it.

Once claimed he preferred doing one-man shows to any other form of theatre, 'because I'm the only person who knows how to give me proper cues.'

Was walking down O'Connell Street one day when he met an acquaintance who gasped, 'Michael – you still have your make-up on you!' The actor replied, 'You scared the life out of me. I thought I'd forgotten to put it on.'

Once saw a sign outside a theatre in Dublin that said, 'This play will be repeated tomorrow night, so those who missed it before will have an opportunity of doing so again.'

When asked if he'd ever slept with a woman he replied, 'I've been accused of many things, but never of being a lesbian.'

Believed it was only a matter of time before an actor as chosen for the role of Hamlet by the size of his penis.

MacMahon, Bryan (1909-98)
Believed the true artist was mad and tried to appear sane, whereas the phoney one was sane and pretended to be mad.

Told of a farmer he knew who came in to money and was able to afford electricity for the first time in his life. 'It's brilliant,' he said, 'I just turn on the light and then I have no problem at all finding the matches for my candles.'

Was a teacher before he became a writer. One day he asked a pupil to name four products that contain milk. He replied, 'Butter, cheese and two cows.'

Another one of his pupils described a zebra as 'a horse with Venetian blinds.'

MacPherson, Ian (1951-)
Hates American politicians who pump up their Gaelic origins to secure the Irish vote. As an example he cites Ronald Reagan, 'who said he was Irish because his great great great great great great grandmother was a fossil under a stone in Galway Bay.'

Says his mother wasn't the traditional Irish mother. Because she was English.

Had a long-term relationship with a Muslim girl. Regretted the fact that he never knew what she looked like.

Macready, R.J.
Believed the best way to pass a cow on the road while cycling was to stay behind it.

Mad Moses
Dublin street character whose hobby was putting plastic bags over the bins. Whenever someone tried to throw something in he'd say, 'You don't really want to throw that away, do you?' The person in question usually came to their senses and abided by Mad Moses' superior wisdom.

Magee, Jimmy (1935-)
Described pigeons as 'symbols of peace' at the opening of the 1982 World Cup.

During a soccer commentary one time, Ireland's famous Memory Man said, 'Jean Tigana has spent the entire first half inside Liam Brady's shorts.'

Mahaffy, Sir John (1839-1919)
Described an Irish atheist as 'Someone who wishes to God he could believe in God. In Ireland, he said, the inevitable never happens but the unexpected occurs constantly.

Makem, Tommy (1932-2007)
Said Catholics were people who sowed their wild oats from Monday to Friday and then went to Mass on Sunday to pray for a crop failure.

Suggesting translating Lady Chatterley's Lover into Irish to facilitate a revival of the language.

Asked once why he was wearing a feather boa he said, 'Since my wife found one in the glove compartment!'

Mallon, Seamus (1936-)
During the troubles the SDLP politician was stopped at a checkpoint by a UDR patrolman who said, 'Good evening, Mr Mallon. What is your name?'

Malone, Paul
Knew a man whose doctor gave him just two weeks to live. The man said, 'Can I have the last week in June and the first one in July?'

Knew another man who thought Freddy Mercury invented the thermometer.

Says there's now a 'new wave' church in California. It has just Three Commandments and Seven Suggestions.

His most noteworthy achievement has been a recording of 'The Fields of Athenry.' Backwards.

Mara, PJ (1942-2015)
According to Eamon Dunphy, Charlie Haughey's former right hand man wore pin-striped short pants as a boy.

Marron, Kevin
The former Sunday World columnist once contemplated setting up an Association for Non-Members. It would have no rules, he said, and would not meet once a month. If anyone asked a non-member for their reaction to the news of

the day, he or she would reply, 'No comment, and don't quote me on that.'

Heard of an ideal type of video machine: It recorded programmes you didn't want to see and showed them when you were out.

Believed the government should nationalise crime – to stop it paying.

Said he left the Irish Press to go into journalism.

Martin, Agnes
Artist who sold a blank canvas to Dublin Corporation cultural committee in October 1980 for £21,000. One councillor (the only sane one?) who opposed the purchase told the committee that buying it was like going into a restaurant, ordering dinner and getting an empty plate.

Mathews, Tom (1952-)
The cartoonist said of a certain village, 'It doesn't have an oldest resident anymore. He died.'

Maturin, Charles Robert (1782-1824)
Clergyman of Huguenot descent who also wrote gothic novels. Was notoriously absent-minded, and was sometimes seen with a boot on one foot and a shoe on the other. Often made social calls in his dressing gown and slippers, or arrived at parties a day late. Served meals to guests and then forgot they were there. Entertained them in conversation until the food went cold.

His most famous novel was *Melmoth the Wanderer*. He sent it to his publishers in seven different parcels and forgot to number the pages. While he was writing it he pasted a wafer onto his forehead as a warning to his family not to interrupt him.

McAlea, Eddie
This hapless thief tried to rob a jewellery store in Limerick in 1980 with a stopper over his gun that stopped it discharging. He was caught after a scuffle and identified by the jeweller, to whom he'd tried to sell his watch the previous day.

McAleer, Kevin (1956-)
The happiest times of his youth, he said, were the hours he spent sitting around the TV set with his family. 'But then, unfortunately, someone would turn it on.'

Is open to the possibility that the 1969 moon landing was faked by John F. Kennedy and Elvis Presley 'so that Marilyn Monroe could be blamed for 9/11.'

Got thrown out of a FCUK shop when he told the manager there was a spelling mistake on the sign.

Blames his irregular heartbeat on being force-fed a diet of irregular verbs in five dead languages as a child.

Believes that in dream language a large brown bear with a Bible on its head means fear of intimacy with an Austrian, while a strong desire to kick the backside of someone who's stubbed out a cigarette in your face is the universal symbol of either drowning slowly in a bath of organic rice or losing your car keys.

When he was in a boarding house one time, his landlady told him to put on a clean pair of socks every day. By the end of the week he couldn't get his feet to fit into his wellingtons.

Two men knocked on his door one day and said, 'We want to talk to you about Jesus.' He said, 'What's he done now?'

McAleese, Mary (1951-)
Sometimes rang pizza shops for a takeaway from the Aras when she was President. They never believed her and often hung up.

McAnally, Ray (1926-89)
Asked a man for directions once. He said, 'You see that road there? Well don't take that.'

McCann, Colum (1965-)
Jumped off a two-storey roof to celebrate winning the 1991 New Writer of the Year Award.

McCann, Donal (1943-99)
When he was on tour with Sean O'Casey's Juno and the Paycock in Jerusalem a journalist asked him how things were going. He said, 'I'm having terrible trouble with my performance because I climbed the Mount of Olives yesterday on a camel and a camel hair lodged in my nostril.' It was nonsense of course but the journalist lapped it up and printed it.

Got so bored while appearing in Diarmuid agus Grainne in the Queen's Theatre in Belfast he decided to insert the word 'elephant' into every other line. Instructed the rest of the cast to do likewise.

Got a taxi to Ardmore Studios in 1993 to shoot The Bishop's Story. Asked the taxi driver to make half a dozen pit-stops along the way for some liquid refreshment in any pub they passed. In each pub he rang the studio to say they'd got a puncture. That was six punctures in thirty miles. When they finally got to the studio the driver handed McCann his 'puncture repair kit' – a packet of mints to kill the smell of liquor.

Asked once by a fan if he was really Donal McCann the famous actor he replied, 'I used to be.'

Was deemed to be 'a bit of Brendan Behan' due to his machismo (and indeed alcoholism) but was brought down to earth one day in a pub by a man who said to him, 'Jaysus, will you look at McCann – the only Irish rebel who goes home every day to his mother for dinner on the 54A bus.'

McCann, Ellen (1785-1889)
Tyrone lady who found her son in a pub when he was 80 and beat him all the way home for his disrespectful conduct. She herself was 104 at the time.

McCann, Sean
Heard of an Irish jury who acquitted a defendant with this verdict: 'We find the man who stole the horse not guilty.'

McCarthy, Daniel (1641-1752)
Kerryman who married five times. The last one was in 1725 when he was 84 and his bride 14. They had 20 children.

McCarthy, Mick (1959-)
Ireland's former manager was as prone to foot-in-mouth disease as most footballers. When a physiotherapist asked him how a torn muscle was doing he said, 'It's a pain in the ass.'

McCarthy, Pete (1951-2004)
Met a man in Manchester who told him he was in a small village in the west of Ireland one night after midnight when

he saw a light on in a bar. He asked a passer-by when the pubs closed. The man replied 'October.'

McCourt, Frank (1930-2009)
Was so poor in childhood that if he woke up on Christmas morning without an erection, he had nothing to play with.

Once saw a reality show about a man whose mother ran off with a giraffe's sister.

The problem with being a writer, he said, is that after you become famous people start asking you about kitchen recipes.

Didn't like Russian novels. 'They go on for 942 pages. On page 920 Boris the peasant decides he wants to commit suicide and you find yourself wishing he did it on page 4.'

McCourt, Malachy (1931-)
Malachy is Frank's brother. It seems to him as if he's spent half his life listening to people saying, 'I read your brother's book.' (That's Angela's Ashes). Is thinking of calling his next book I Read Your Brother's Book.

Once auditioned for the part of an Irish priest in a film but was informed he didn't have the right accent for it.

Said he was educated in a school for emotionally disturbed teachers.

McDaid, Marguerite
Wrote a book about being married to the politician Jim McDaid. Said one of the reasons the marriage collapsed was because she could never get his shirts as white as his teeth.

McDermott, Joe
Soccer fan with a colourful past that includes haggling with the KGB, lying to the CID, fighting with Vietnamese veterans, dancing with Zulu warriors, walking up Mount Vesuvius with three drunken Chinamen, praying with nuns in the Vatican, sleeping with winos in New York, falling of a train in Norway, reciting poetry in Los Angeles, getting a job as a wages clerk for Clint Eastwood, playing basketball with the Harlem Globetrotters, meeting Diego Maradona, posing as a musketeer in Amsterdam... and being barred from every flight leaving Britain for a year. When he was heading off to an Irish soccer international in 1983 he downed eight pints of beer and a few whiskies. At Luton airport he got into a fight with some English men and ended up in jail. The next morning in court the judge looked at his clothes, which were painted green, white and gold, and said to him: 'Having you nothing better to wear?' McDermott replied, 'Jaysus, Your Honour, I was just about to ask you the same question.'

McEvoy, Johnny (1945-)
The singer had suffered from bi-polar depression for most of his life, which has resulted in brief periods of manic energy followed by longer bouts of exhaustion and dark moods. Asked by an interviewer how his family found out about his illness, he replied, 'When they saw me out mowing the lawn one morning at five a.m.!'

McEvoy, Mary (1954-)
Says she lost her virginity purely (impurely?) to get rid of it.

Hates being small. Thought of suing the County Council for building the road so close to her arse.

McFadden, Bryan (1980-)
His name was originally spelt 'Brian'. He changed it, he said, because he had to sign a lot of autographs when he was with Westlife and it was too cumbersome lifting the pen from the page to dot the 'i'.

Gave up the idea of studying law because he doesn't like reading books. 'That could have been a problem,' he allows.

Is so lazy he finds changing TV channels with the remote a chore. Wouldn't wash a dish to save his life.

McGaha, Kris
This man is of Dutch Irish extraction, 'which means that my idea of a good time is to get drunk and drive my car into a windmill.'

McGahern, John (1934-2006)
The acclaimed novelist immersed himself in his work so much his sisters often stood behind him for ages as he sat in his chair without him being aware of them being in the room.

Believed some books must 'long for the death of their writers so they could assume a life of their own.'

Said his favourite optimist was a man who threw himself off the Empire State building. As he passed the 42nd floor he was heard to say, 'So far so good.'

Felt one of the consolations of heaven, if he ever got there, would be that there wouldn't be many writers around.

Was sacked from his teaching post in the 1960s after writing The Dark, which was regarded as a 'dirty' book (it was actually a very beautiful one) and marrying a Finnish woman in a registry office while on a career break. 'It was an Irish sacking,' said McGahern, 'Nobody would actually say my job was gone.' To force the authorities to come out of the closet, McGahern reported to work every day as normal, drinking 'endless cups of tea' in the staff room but having no class to teach. Eventually the parish priest called him up to his house to formally advise him of the termination of his employment. 'If it was only the oul' book I could probably have done something about it,' he said, 'But why did you have to go off and marry a foreign woman when there are so many lovely Irish girls with their tongues hanging out for a husband?' McGahern was nonplussed, 'If there were,' he said, 'I never saw them hanging out in my direction.'

McGahon, Brendan (1936-)
Outspoken politician who outraged the gay community when he said homosexuals were 'abnormal', had persecution complexes and were to be compared with 'left-handed drivers trying to drive on the right-hand side of the road. (There was, however, no truth in the rumour that he wanted them to be castrated with dirty nails).

McGee Eugene
The footballer trainer lists the following excuse as the best he ever got from a player who failed to turn up at one of his workouts: 'The wheel fell off my mobile phone.'

McGinty, Thom (1952-1995)
Aka The Diceman, McGinty was Scots by birth but he lived in Ireland from the 1970s to the end of his life. He stood motionless on Grafton Street most days, painted up like a clown. Other guises included a teapot, a bulb and a condom. Was arrested once for wearing a skimpy loin cloth that failed

to cover his buttocks. Other times he was asked to 'move on' by the police, something he did so slowly, very few people could see him actually moving. Was once reputed to have gone the whole length of Grafton Street without appearing to move. If you dropped some money at his feet, though, he might give you one of his trademark winks.

Died of HIV in 1995 and was widely mourned. His coffin was carried down Grafton Street to wide applause. This time, for a change, the movement was obvious.

McGuigan, Barry (1961-)
After fighting Nicky Perez he said, 'I missed him with some tremendous punches. The wind from them could have given him pneumonia.'

Is a native of Clones, 'the town where everybody looks like me.'

Said he was the only boxer in his family: 'All the others are Alsatians.'

McKeever, Kevin
Cash-strapped property developer who was found rambling on a country road in Leitrim in January 2015 looking the worse for wear. He told police he'd been kidnapped and held hostage for the previous eight months, being fed on little but ham sandwiches. His story was eventually discovered to be a hoax and he was arrested for wasting police time. His motive for the ruse? A desperate need to escape his creditors.

McKenna, T.P. (1929-2011)
Once heard of an Irishman who killed himself to get revenge on the Samaritans for taking him off their danger list.

McKeon, Sean
Wrote a book in which he relates the following events in his adventurous life:

His mother was seven hours in labour because the nurses forgot to take her tights off.

He was breastfed by his father.

Was kept in High Infants so long, his teacher wanted to adopt him.

The only thing he passed at school was worms.

The town he grew up in was so conservative, the local prostitute was a virgin.

The first time he went to the zoo and saw a zebra he thought it was one of his father's donkeys in pyjamas.

Got a yellow belt in karate.

McNamara, John
Won the first frog-swallowing championship of Ireland at Ballycomber, Offaly in 1975. He managed to swallow five live frogs in a minute and five seconds.

McNeice, Louis (1907-63)
Became so drunk at the funeral of Dylan Thomas he threw a bunch of sandwiches onto the coffin imagining they were flowers.

McSavage, David (1965-)
Thanks happiness makes the Irish feel sad.

Decided he wanted to break it off with his girlfriend when he heard her tidying the cabinets in his kitchen.

McWilliams, David (1966-)
Before Sex and the City he thought 'A Brazilian' was a footballer.

Ever since the recession, he says, it's become more trendy to be seen in Woodies than Lillie's.

Meaney, Mike
Ballyporeen man who allowed himself to be buried in a closed casket under a pub in Kilburn for 61 days in 1968.

Mee, Michael
Describes himself as 'a pacifist by physique.'

Miley, Jimmy
When this Wicklow Councillor heard of a scheme to put gondolas on Blessington Lake he said, 'That's all very well but who's going to feed them?'

Milligan, Spike (1918-2001)
Believed the best cure for seasickness was to sit under a tree.

Said his father had a profound influence on him: 'He was a lunatic.'

His father was shellshocked in the war. He used to come home every night, take out a pistol and shout at the parlour door, 'If you're in there Hitler, come out with your hands up.'

A reporter saw him looking approvingly at a tree one day and asked him what he was thinking. 'I was thinking I love that tree,' he said, 'because I don't have to make it laugh.'

Believed the army works like this: If a man dies when you hang him, keep on doing it until he gets used to it.

During a game of rugby one time he handed the ball to an overzealous member of the opposing team with the words, 'Is this what you were looking for?'

When an army doctor told him to take off his clothes for a medical examination he said, 'Shouldn't you take me out to dinner first?'

For a lot of his life he thought an innuendo was an Italian suppository.

Saw a sign on a lift one time that said, 'Please do not use this when it is not working.'

Didn't classify himself as a snob but still wore a bowler hat when he took a bath: 'You never know who might call.'

Stabbed Peter Sellers with a potato knife to get himself admitted to a psychiatric hospital.

Once asked a Soho prostitute who were her best and worst customers. 'The English are the best,' she said, 'because they're so ashamed of what they're doing they want to get in and out as quickly as possible. The Irish are the worst because they want to kiss us as well.'

Leaped onto the conveyor belt at an airport as the luggage was coming through. When an official gazed disapprovingly at him he said, 'Just one more round and I promise to get off. I've wanted to do this all my life.'

Wanted his gravestone to say, 'I told you I was sick.'

When he looked back on his life, he mused in old age, his fondest memories weren't of The Goons or other stellar heights he reached. They were of a girl called Julia with enormous breasts.

Saint Mochua
Used a pet fly as a bookmark for his hymn books.

Monaghan, David
This comedian's father is Irish and his mother is Iranian. He says he spent most of his family holidays in Customs.

Monckton, Mary (1746-1840)
Monckton was the wife of the 7th Earl of Cork. She suffered from kleptomania. Whenever she was invited anywhere she helped herself to whatever she could get her hands on. One time she even nicked a live hedgehog from a venue, dropping it into her handbag before making off home.

Moore, Christy (1945-)
Asked why he sang so often with his eyes closed, gave the explanation, 'Because the words of the songs are written on the inside of my eyelids.'

Discounts the pernicious rumour that he only knows three chords. 'I actually know four,' he insists.

Believes there are only three questions that really matter in life: Who made the world? Would you have the price of a drink? Can I stay at your gaff tonight?

Moore, George (1852-1933)
Said his one claim to fame among Irishmen was that he never made a speech.

Defined an Irish literary movement as 'half a dozen writers who cordially detest one another.'

Attributed his long life to the fact that he never smoked, drank or touched a girl... until he was ten.

Oscar Wilde said of him, 'He leads his readers to the latrine and locks them in.'

Moran, Dylan (1971-)
The stand-up comic can't drive. He was going to learn but can't swim either and was afraid he might drive into a lake.

Thinks Ireland has changed markedly in recent times: 'When I was growing up, my relatives had four teeth between them. Now everyone is dating somebody called Pegrovia.'

Believes we measure how good a time we had on a night out in Ireland by how badly we feel the next morning. 'How did you get on last night?' 'Brilliant. I can't see.'

Life is simple for men, he says. When they're children they have one finger up their nose and the other on their penis. 'Then we get taller.'

The difference between men and women, he thinks, is that women use headaches to stop having sex while men use sex to stop having headaches.

Thinks German sounds like tin foil being eaten by a typewriter as it's being kicked down the stairs.

Doesn't see himself as a good fighter because he bleeds too much. His best chance of victory in any encounter, he thinks, would be to drown his opponent in his own blood.

Believes that if genitalia could sing, they'd sound like Enya.

Doesn't take drugs anymore. If he wants a thrill he simply stands up suddenly.

Is looking forward to being really old so he can lean over in a restaurant and say to his son, 'I just pissed myself. Deal with it.'

Morgan, Dermot (1952-98)
Believed the ideal wife for an Irishman was a rich nymphomaniac who lived in a pub over a racecourse and turned into a pizza after sex.

Defined confession as 'a rare and wonderful opportunity to be able to go in and talk dirty to a total stranger.'

The next nuclear war will be held in London, he said once, so England won't have to qualify.

Died suddenly in 1998. Afterwards Peter Howick said, 'I couldn't tell you where Dermot is now but wherever he is, Dermot didn't believe in it.'

Morley, John
The former Mayo footballer said he was always getting criticised for using his right foot, 'but without it I couldn't use my left one.'

Morrissey, Eamon (1943-)
Was giving his one-man show The Brother at the Peacock once while Chekhov's Three Sisters was playing at the Abbey. Both theatres had the same phone number. A woman rang up for seats. She was asked if they were for Three Sisters or The Brother. 'What are you talking about?' she said, 'They're for myself and my cousin.'

Mortimer, Pauline
This Dublin lass won a marathon in 1981 at the age of 14. Her achievement? She spent over eight hours cleaning her teeth. Her mother promised her a new toothbrush afterwards.

Mullinahack
This was the nickname of a beggar who roamed around the streets of Dublin in the 1940s. Whenever anyone gave him a penny he'd shout, for reasons best know to himself, 'They'll never bate the Chinese out of Mullinahack!'

Mumba, Samantha (1983-)
Wanted fame so badly, she said, she'd have run across a football pitch naked to achieve it.

Murray, Patrick
Said he had nothing against Jesuits but wouldn't have wanted his daughter to marry one.

Murdoch, Iris (1899-1985)
Believed a bad review of a book was less important than if it was raining in Patagonia.

Murphy, Colin (1968-)
Came from a broken home. He broke it.

Believes the smoking ban in pubs denied people one of the greatest pleasures known to man: chasing a butt down a trough for thirty seconds while urinating.

Murphy, Mike (1941-)
Says his pet hate was people asking him what his pet hate was.

Likes to correct the false allegation people have put about that he didn't get his Leaving Cert: 'It was my Inter I didn't get.'

Murtie, Kevin
Left this note for his milkman one morning: 'No milk today. By today I mean tomorrow as I wrote this yesterday.'

Myers, Kevin (1947-)
When he watches golf he has roughly the same sensation the pharaohs of ancient Egypt had when forceps were inserted through their nostrils to pull their brains down from their skulls.

Nolan, Finbar (1945-)
This healer is the seventh son of a seventh son. He says arthritis and rheumatism are caused by a worm in the spine. When he was two, he says, his mother put a worm in his hand and it died instantly.

Nolan, Philip
Believe Germans only do two things well – Christmas and surrendering.

Norris, David (1944-)
His greatest ambition, next to bring President of Ireland, was to marry the Pope, have 2.7 kids, divorce him on grounds of

mental cruelty, win custody of the two kids and leave him to change the nappy on the remining .7 one.

Norton, Graham (1963-   )
Believes thunder is God trying to parallel park.

Heard of a couple who were so liberal they wanted to adopt a gay baby.

The Nualas
Wore 'soundproof knickers' when they were on stage to cover up the ticking of their body clocks.

Their most famous pronouncement was when Bernie shouted at an under-appreciative audience, 'Clap your feet.'

O'Brien, Cornelius (1872-   )
Liscannor MP who was regarded as one of the best Ireland ever had because he didn't open his mouth for his twenty years in office.

O'Briain, Dara (1972-   )
Describes himself as being 'ethnically Catholic': 'Don't believe in God, still hate Rangers.'

O'Brien, Edna (1930-   )
Wrote her first novel at the age of eight.

Says she's attracted to 'thin, tall, Good-looking men who have one common denominator. They must be lurking bastards.'

Spent all night with Marlon Brando in her flat in London one night in the 1960s. He didn't sleep with her, surprisingly enough, but spent most of the night talking to her instead.

He told her he had one important question to ask her and waited ages before telling her what it was. He unleashed it as he pushed her up and down on a bucket swing in a park the following morning: 'Are you ticklish?'

O'Brien, Flann (1911-66)
Believed the typical Irish family consisted of father, mother, twelve children and resident Dutch anthropologist.

Believed bicycles could have sex with one another – though not, ideally, on a first date.

Thought reality was an illusion generated by the insufficiency of alcohol.

Avoided a drink driving conviction by sitting drunk inside a car that had no engine in it. Another night in a police station he happily slurped a bottle of whiskey in front of a Garda, thereby negating the effect of a blood test.

Claimed to be a lapsed agnostic.

Didn't think it was necessarily a bad thing that we weren't the people our fathers were. Because if we were we would probably be very old.

O'Brien, Pat (1899-1983)
'I've played so many priests in films,' he said, 'when my family and myself sit down to eat, we speak Italian.'

His housekeeper was a Baptist. His family doctor was a Jew. His lawyer was a Congregationalist, his secretary a presbyterian and his wife a convert. He had four Catholic children and six Catholic grandchildren. 'I'm looking for some atheist friends,' he pleaded.

O'Brien, Tim
Holiday agent who was also a member of a group he called The Irish Society for the Abolition of Sex. He advertised 'sexless' holidays in the Curragh, Ballymurphy and Croagh Patrick in the 1970s stating that people were 'fed up of sun, sea and squelching vacations.' He offered an alternative. To cool the holiday-makers' ardour, he recommended ice-cold showers and bouts of nettle-whipping.

O'Carroll, Brendan (1955-)
His family was so poor that one Christmas when he asked for a yo-yo, all he got was a piece of string. His father told him it was a yo.

The school he went to was so tough, he says, the arms of the chairs even had tattoos on them.

Used to know a man who was so lazy he'd sit in front of the fire and cry out, 'Help – I'm burning!'

Once made love to a woman from 11.55 to 1.03. He thinks that was the night the clocks went forward.

His wife failed to turn up at his first one-man show in the Olympia preferring to take her mother to Bingo instead.

When he asked his wife what she'd like for Christmas one year she said, 'Something with diamonds,' so he bought her a pack of cards.

Gave up smoking for lent one year. Said it was the longest hour of his life.

When his wife asked him to buy her something with diamonds he got her a deck of cards.

Wants to write an Irish trilogy. That's one with four books in it.

Believed Anna Kournikova's decision to retire from tennis was on a par with Bono's decision to give up acting. Felt she would probably have a more promising career as a Russian novelist.

Says his grandson is named after the two Irish Popes: Bono and John Paul.

Agrees that Nicorette is the best cure for nicotine addiction: 'Just put a patch over each eye and you won't be able to find your cigarettes.'

O'Conaire, Padraig (1881-1928)
At the time of his death his only belongings were a pipe, some tobacco and an apple.

O'Connell, Brian
Got so drunk in 1991 he thought he was a fighter pilot singing U2's 'One' while bombarding the urban sprawl of Dublin with the remnants of a snack box from Enzo's takeaway.

O'Connell, Paddy
Clare man who lived in Fiji for forty years in the 19th century, managing to father 48 children in that time.

O'Connor, Christy (1924-)
'If golf wasn't my living,' he famously remarked, 'I wouldn't play it if you paid me.'

Once hit a tee shot deliberately into the trees. 'There was method in my madness,' he said, 'I was suffering from a hangover and a friend of mine was in there with a flask of coffee and a hair of the dog.'

O'Connor, Frank (1903-66)
O'Connor was a librarian as well as a writer. One day a man came into the library where he worked and said he wanted to complain about an indecent book he's seen there on a previous visit. Asked what was indecent about it, he said there was a 'dirty word' on Page 164. O'Connor got the book and asked him to point to the word. The man pointed to 'navel.'

O'Connor, Joseph (1963-)
When O'Connor was asked what he considered to be the most important quality a writer should possess, he answered: 'A certain quality of stupidity.'

Said one of the most pleasing experiences in his life was managing to write 'Yeats' and 'fuck' in the same sentence.

Tried to French-kiss a girl in a Gaeltacht once but got his tongue caught in her dental brace.

Heard of a couple aged 90 and 91 respectively who were about to divorce. Asked by a reporter why they'd waited so long, they replied, 'We were waiting for the children to die.'

O'Connor, Michael
Irish shop assistant who emigrated to Australia in the early years of the last century. In 1907 he was arrested in Melbourne for impulsively throwing his arms around an unknown customer and kissing her passionately. His defence

was that he was in high spirits because it was a lovely spring day. This was thrown out and he was imprisoned for a breach of the peace. Then years later, O'Connor received a call from his solicitor to say that the lady in question, one Hazel Moore, had died and left him £20,000 in her will – in memory of the only time in her life she'd ever been kissed by a man.

O'Connor, Richard
Believes the most attractive house for a burglar to rob is one with an alarm going off. 'Because everyone always ignores them.'

Defines old age as being stuck in a traffic jam and thinking, 'Thank God I don't have to pee.'

O'Connor, Sinead (1967-2023)
When she was young she thought she was the reincarnation of St. Bernadette.

Shaved her hair off, she said, because someone confused her with Enya.

Was ordained to the priesthood in 1999 by a rebel bishop. Shortly afterwards she declared that she was bisexual.

Has a love-hate relationship with Ireland. 'It's a country,' she feels, 'that needs to be dragged into a bush and fucked.'

Tore up a photograph of the Pope on Saturday Night Live in 1992 as a protest at the child abuse scandals in the church. A later Saturday Night Live show parodied the action by having an actor dressed up as the Pope tearing up a photo of O'Connor. Her brother Joseph says he sent him the photo with an apology and a big roll of Sellotape: 'I got a nice postcard back. Since then we've kept in touch.'

O'Connor, Ulick (1928-)
Says Irish Alzheimer patients forget 'everything but the grudges'. Samuel Beckett might have agreed. ('Let me say before I die that I forgive nobody').

O'Dea, Jimmy (1899-1965)
Stopped drinking coffee in the morning because it kept him awake all day.

O'Doherty, Ian
Believes women who have breast implants should be sued under the Advertising Standards Act.

O'Donnell, Daniel (1961-)
The singer isn't as tame as people think. Once, for instance, he's reputed to have eaten his After-8 mints at 7.30. And on another occasion he crossed his legs without looking left or right.

Took tea without milk one day at Kincasslagh. Magella refrained from calling the Security Forces.

O'Donnell, Liz (1956-)
When she told her husband she was thinking of running for politics he said, 'That's grounds for annulment.'

O'Donnell, Turlough (? – 1423)
The Lord of Tyrconnell, as he was called, fathered 18 sons by ten different women. He had 59 grandsons.

O'Donoghue, John
This man sold a house to Twink that had a smaller house on its grounds which he built for the express purpose of putting his Rolls-Royce in it. She eventually moved her parents into it.

O'Dowd, Dan
Wannabe doctor who asked his Career Guidance Officer how he might get into Medical College. He received the reply, 'Donate your body to science.'

O'hEochagain, Hector (1969-)
Doesn't care what people say about him as long as they spell his name wrong.

O'Faolain, Nuala (1940-2008)
After she contracted cancer in 2008 she did a radio interview with Marian Finucane in which she said, 'There's nothing wrong with me apart from the fact that I'm dying.'

O'Faolain, Sean (1900-91)
This scribe wrote hundreds of thousands of words but is perhaps best remembered for one tiny epigram: 'An Irish queer is a man who prefers women to drink.'

Believed the bottom of a whiskey bottle was too near the top.

O'Farrell, John
O'Farrell's mother stoutly resisted the blandishments of technology but he was determined to get her to change her ways. After many efforts to persuade her to use emails instead of her preferred penmanship when writing to him, she finally sat down at the computer he'd bought for her and wrote him an email.

She then printed it out, stuck it in an envelope and sent it to him.

O'Flynn, Gary
Former City Councillor who pleaded guilty to three counts of soliciting murder in July 2015. The people he wished to see dispatched to their happy hunting grounds were an accountant, a detective and a revenue commissioner.

Ogle, John
Colonel who walked all the way from Dublin to Dundalk, a distance of 53 miles, to win a bet in 1797. The best was for... a penny.

O'Grady, Paul (1955-2023)
Was on so many pills throughout his life he thought he'd be buried in a coffin with a child-proof lid.

The latest thing in men's clothes, he once said, was women.

O'Hanlon, Ardal (1965-)
The former Fr Ted star always harboured an ambition to interview Neil Armstrong, and to ask him about everything but his moon walk.

Describes himself as a dancer trapped in the body of a tree.

Doesn't think he'd have made a good suicide bomber. 'They're promised 72 virgins. One would do me.'

Said there were only three occasions at which his family always convened: weddings, funerals and when he bought home chips.

Always hated when his father carried him on his shoulders as a child. Especially when they were in the car.

O'Hanlon, Ellis (1965-)
Says John Wayne Bobbit is now dating a bulimic: 'She can't keep anything down and he can't keep anything up.'

O'Hara, Maureen (1920-2015)
Was never hot copy for the Hollywood tabloids. 'I was too normal,' she confessed, 'I didn't give my baby away, or paint my face green on Paddy's Day. And I got to work on time. So un-Irish.'

Married a man in England after going on just two dates with him. Left for America the following day. Never saw him again.

Her second husband was alcoholic. At one time she thought he was trying to murder her.

Believed the death of her third husband in a plane crash could have been 'arranged.'

O'Hempsey, Denis (1697-1807)
Blind harpist who managed the unusual feat of straddling three different centuries. He put his longevity down to healthy living, lots of exercise and a diet of milk, water and potatoes. He married at the relatively young age (for him) 86 and fathered a child the following year. Was walking up to four months before his death.

O'Kane, Deirdre (1970-)
Describes herself as a jaded individual. Says she came out of the womb, took one look around and said to her mother, 'Is that it?'

Was fired from a job as a waitress when a diner asked her what marinated mushrooms were and she said, 'They're mushrooms that grow by the sea.'

Thinks the problem with drink in Ireland is that a problem with it isn't considered a problem by the person who has the problem. If other people have a problem about that, that's their problem.

Saw a sign on a church recently that said, 'We're open on Sundays now.'

Thinks Irish people can't take compliments. If you tell them they look well they say, 'How could I? Wasn't I just kicked in the head by a bullock?'

O'Keeffe, Martin
Is a confessed 'paranoid dyslexic'. In other words he believes Marily Monroe wasn't killed by the CIA but rather the ICA – the Irish Countrywoman's Association.

O'Keeffe, Michael
When he realised the truth of the dictum that 'It's always the last place you look' when you lose something, has now decided to look in the last place first.

O'Keeffe, Susan
Describes herself as a nymphomaniac, hypochondriac, anorexic, suicidal, demonic, perverse, racist psychotic sociopath with delusions of grandeur.

O'Kelly, Dennis (1728-87)
This gentleman taught his pet parrot to whistle the 104th Psalm.

O'Kelly, Derek
Relates an anecdote in his book 'What's the Story?' about the craic that was had in Mountjoy Prison during the 1990 World Cup when drink was smuggled in, bedsheets converted into tricolours and headbands and scarves worn by all the inmates as they watched the matches on television. So great was the mirth that one prisoner who was out on parole returned to his cell two days early.

O'Leary, David (1958-)
The former Irish international offered this insight into his childhood to an interviewer: 'I was a young lad when I was growing up.'

Asked what he thought of the referee of a match on which he'd just commentated he said, 'The decisions decided a lot of things but I'll leave that for other people to decide.'

O'Leary, Michael (1961-)
In 2009 the Ryanair boss considered charging people a euro to go to the toilet. He also considered imposing an extra levy on overweight people. Passengers on Ryanair were asked to log on to a website and choose from four possible options on how such a levy could be applied. The options were: (1) A charge per kilogram for males over 130kg and females over 100kg; (2) A charge per inch for every waistline over 45 inches for men and 40 inches for women; (3) A charge for every point in excess of 40 points in the Body Mass Index; or (4) A charge for a second seat if a passenger's waist touched two armrests simultaneously. The stratagem caused one passenger to remark, 'If two people are thin enough to fit on a seat, will they get it for half price?'

O'Leary's ruthless cost-cutting manoeuvres caused another passenger to groan, 'When is he going to ask us to bring our own parachutes?' Says Ardal O'Hanlon, 'Pilots will be the next thing to go. He'll just get these giant catapults and fire people in the general direction of their destination.'

O'Mahony, Eoin
Said his entire involvement with the Irish Literary Revival consisted of standing beside W.B. Yeats one night during an interval at the Abbey where he remembered the poet having great difficulty with his waterworks.

O'Mahony, Tim
Vet fined for drunken driving some years ago in Macroom. Asked why he had whiskey in his car he explained, 'I don't normally drink it. I keep it there in case I encounter any calves suffering from pneumonia.'

O'Neill Stratford, Benjamin
This gentleman had an ambition to build the world's biggest balloon in a huge barn in the 1930s. His dream died after twenty years of trying when the barn caught fire and destroyed the balloon. Inconsolable, he emigrated to Spain and lived in a run-down hotel where he had all his meals delivered to his room. When the unwashed crockery became too much for him to bear, he simply changed rooms.

O'Neill, Eugene (1888-1953)b
Wrote a will in the voice of his dog Silverdene in which he bequeathed his 'loved and faith' to his master and mistress because dogs were not like humans in the amassing of material things so he had nothing else to leave. He asked them to remember him fondly but not to grieve unduly and not let his passing stop them from having other pets.

O'Neill, Martin (1952-)
When he was managing Celtic he remarked after a UEFA Cup defeat: 'It's a dreadful disappointment but the players have nothing to be disappointed about.'

O'Neill, Owen
This Belfast man was asked 'What's the name of the place that's always being bombed?' 'I don't know', he replied, 'It's not there any more.'

When he told a foreigner he was from Belfast, the man said, 'Is that near anywhere else?'

O'Neill, Patricia (1924-2012)b
Daughter of the Countess of Kenmare who wrote her husband Frank out of her will in 2000 after deciding to leave her fortune to her pet chimp Kalu instead. The chimp, whose favourite hobby was bashing Frank over the head, would have inherited £30 million. Patricia had 48 chimps in all, as well as 22 baboons, many of whom shared her bed to facilitate night feeds. Kalu also liked to smoke Frank's cigarettes and drink his beer from the fridge. She felt that by leaving all her money to him she'd stop Frank from mistreating him after she died but she lost her fortune and Kalu had to deal with living just as thriftily as all the other chimps he knew.

O'Regan, Colm
Was on the street one day when a man came up to him and said, 'I thought you were someone else.' O'Regan replied, 'I am.'

O'Reilly, Jane
Says the only thing her husband ever achieved on his own was his moustache.

O'Reilly, Tony (1936-)
Played rugby for Ireland before he became a newspaper magnate. Said the average training session in the 1970s involved 'running around Barry McGann twice.'

Osborne, Jonathan (1794-1864)
Dublin physician who asked to be buried in an upright coffin as he didn't want anyone to have an advantage over him at the resurrection.

O'Sullivan, Maureen (1911-98)
O'Sullivan appeared as Jane in a number of Tarzan films. She complained that Cheetah, Tarzan's favourite ape, used to bite her repeatedly because 'The Tarzan apes were always very eager to wrap their paws around Johnny Weissmuller's thighs. They were jealous of me and I loathed them. They were all homosexuals.'

O'Toole, Joe (1947-)
Says people in Ireland hate growing old more than dying.

O'Toole, Peter (1932-2013)
Said he was the only actor (person?) in the world whose two names were synonyms for 'penis.'

Was superstitious right through his life. Also never wore a watch, never carried a wallet and never took his keys with him when he was out of the house: 'I just hope some bastard's in.' (On one occasion when they weren't, he had to explain to a passing policeman why he was breaking into his own house).

Wrote off two cars speeding. In the opinion of a friend, the 'Lawrence of Arabia' star was 'better at riding camels than driving cars.'

Engaged in legendary binges during his acting days. One day a theatrical co-star said to him, 'Do you know what act we're in?' O'Toole replied, 'Never mind that. What bloody play are we in?'

Claimed to have gone for a beer one night in Paris and woke up in Corsica.

Stayed at a grotty flat in London with Richard Harris for a time. The pair of them were peckish and looked in the fridge for something to eat. They saw what looked like a suspicious looking pork chop so decided to take a raincheck on it. They threw it out the window and decided to have some whiskey instead. The next morning they looked out the window and saw a dead dog beside the so-called chop. Was it really a chop? O'Toole thought it now looked more like a dead cat. 'Just as well we didn't eat it,' he said to Harris. Harris nodded uncertainly.

Decided to buy a pub one night because he was refused a drink in it.

Realised he was God the day he started praying and discovered he was talking to himself.

Paisley, Rev. Ian (1926-2014)
Blamed the Anglo-Irish Agreement for Sunday drinking.

Believed St Patrick was a Protestant.

Parnell, Charles Stewart (1846-91)
Parnell was so superstitious, every time he walked from him driveway to his house he felt it was bad luck if the number of footsteps he took ended in multiples of four. If they did he walked back to the driveway and walked down again, this time taking longer or shorter strides.

Often wore two overcoats, as can be seen in the statue of him at the end of Parnell Street.

Said to a parliamentary meeting once, 'It seems unanimous we can't agree.'

Penn, Sean (1960-)
Met a man in a pub in Dublin one night who told him he should never have married Maradona.

Perrot, John
Waterford Evangelist who visited Rome in 1658 to try and convert Pope Alexander VII to the Quaker faith. He didn't succeed and was thrown in prison instead.

Pockrich, Richard (1695-1759)
Musician whose most famous invention was musical glasses. He created notes by tapping adjoining ones intermittently. So entranced was he with his 'angelic organ', he played it once for bailiffs who came to arrest him for outstanding debts. They were sufficiently impressed to cancel the debts.

Tuned his glasses by putting different levels of water in them. The tones were brought out by passing his fingers around the brims.

Subsequently considered forming an orchestra which was to be comprised of just one person, playing various-sized drums. Another of his many ideas was raising geese on barren terrain in Wicklow.

He was also a political animal and lobbied the Irish Parliament for a directive that involved draining the bogs and replacing them with vineyards. Despite such genius, however, he failed in two attempts to fun for government.

Pockrich believed life could be extended by repeated blood transfusions. He believed that if the 'redundant' blood of old people was mixed with the 'vibrant' blood of the young, life expectancy could be unlimited. He agreed, however, that if an individual attained the age of 999, it was only fair that he or she should be declared 'legally dead' and an Act of Parliament decree that their assets accede to their descendants.

His musical prowess was eventually recognised in 1741, at which time entertained guests in his rooms by tapping on his glasses with wooden spoons and occasionally even allowing a singer to accompany him. Afterwards he toured Ireland and England entertaining audiences with the works of Handel and others in this way.

A man of many parts, Pockrich also published a collection of poetry, and tried to persuade parliament to link the Liffey and the Shannon by a series of canals. More prosaically, he recommended people try to keep their wrinkles at bay by steeping brown paper in vinegar and applying it to the face at half-hour intervals.

Potter, Maureen (1925-2004)
Once told a dentist she'd prefer to have a baby than have a tooth out. He said she'd have to make up her mind before he adjusted the chair.

Believed people weren't supposed to look happy while doing Irish dancing.

At 71 she said she got a standing ovation for just standing.

Pound Note
This was the sobriquet of a man who walked the streets of Dublin in the rare old times, picking up pieces of paper and stuffing them into his pockets until he had so many he could hardly move. The story goes that he found a pound note on a pavement one day and lived the rest of his life in the hope that history would repeat itself.

Power, John
Former executive of the Irish Hotels Federation who was shocked by the fact that in 2004 the international health care group Bupa refused to hold a major conference in Dublin because of its smoking ban. 'It re-located to Britain,' said Power, 'where delegates didn't have to leave the building to smoke.'

Prone, Terry
When she cooks, she says, the kitchen looks like a deranged bison that's been salsa dancing on the work surface.

Purcell, Noel (1900-85)
Knew a woman who gave her dentures back to the dentist. She said they wouldn't fit in the glass she kept on her bedside locker.

Said his father discovered a cure for amnesia but couldn't remember what it was.

Read in a book that smoking was bad for you, so gave up reading.

Lost his index finger in an accident with a circular saw. 'It meant I could never play the violin again,' he said, adding, 'But – as I never played it in the first place that didn't bother me too much.'

When a friend of Purcell's told him he looked tired one day, he said, 'I was up half the night waiting for the cat to come in so I could let her out.'

Purser, Saray (1848-1943)
Held her first art exhibition at 75.

At the age of 89 she asked Oliver St. John Gogarty for a trip in his plane. She wanted to have a look at the roof of Mespil House, where she was living at the time.

Died of shock after seeing a poor portrait of Douglas Hyde.

Quinn, Anthony (1915-2000)
Quinn came from a colourful lineage, including an Irish father. He said his ambition in life was to be Picasso, Martin Luther, Jack Dempsey, Shakespeare, Michelangelo and Shakespeare and Napoleon rolled into one.

He used to run backwards for half a mile every day as a young man when he briefly contemplated a career as a boxer.

Nearly strangled his wife one night after waking up from a nightmare, imaging her to be a panther about to devour him.

Slapped her on their wedding night when he found out she wasn't a virgin.

Quinn, Niall (1966-)
Said once of a spectacular goal: 'It was the sort of shot that made your hair stand on your shoulders.'

Quinlan, Ronan
Describes himself as a Catholic atheist rather than a Protestant one.

Redmond, Michael (1950-)
Was born Catholic, which came as a bit of a shock to his parents, who are both Jewish.

Never liked it when his grandfather visited, because he was told he had his eyes. And he was blind.

Says his grandfather died in his rocking chair: 'I was five. I didn't know it would keel over when I climbed on his back.'

Remembered family evenings around the fire in childhood. His father would be fretting about the coming harvest and his mother would be telling him not to worry about things like that. Because he was an accountant.

Once ate a tin of dogfood for a bet. Lost the bet because he'd bet that he *wouldn't* eat it.

Used to gatecrash funerals for the free booze. One day a woman discovered he wasn't connected to the deceased and asked him to leave. 'With an attitude like that,' he told her, 'you'll never make friends.'

Likes going into sweet shops and saying, 'Excuse me, is that Mars bar for sale?' When they say 'Yes', he says, 'Okay, I might be back later. I have a few other ones to see first.'

Went to a furniture shop with his wife to buy a coffee table. They couldn't see one they both liked so they compromised and bought one they both hated instead.

Stopped caring about passing his driving test when he did it the '44th' time. The examiner said to him, 'I thought I told you to turn right there.' He replied, 'You did, but I'm going to Wales instead to visit my sister. I told her I'd have a friend with me.'

Likes sitting in the smoking section of restaurants and going up to non-smokers to tell them they should be smoking.

Rice, Edmund (1762-1844)
Had the good sense to wait until his wife died before forming the Christian Brothers, an organisation comprised totally of bachelors.

Roach, Hal (1927-2012)
Had 46-inch hips before he started drinking low fat milk. Afterwards he had 46-inch knees.

Believed the most difficult years of marriage were those following the wedding.

Defined a health addict as someone who ate health food so he wouldn't ruin his health and have to eat health food.

A babysitter told him one that a good way to keep a baby quiet was to get it to suck on a bottle of glue.

Communism as a philosophy bothered him: 'They have nothing and they want to share it with us.'

Finally found a diet that works in Ireland: 'I only eat when the weather is good.'

Robinson, Lennox (1888-1958)
When the playwright had too many sherries he became confused. One night he queued for two hours to sing the Bing Crosby film 'Going My Way' under the impression that he was standing in the queue for the tram to Dalkey.

Robinson, Matthew (1712-1800)
Also known as Lord Rokeby, Robinson hated shaving so much he grew a beard down to his knees. He also had an obsession with swimming, sometimes staying in the water so long he fainted and had to be rescued by his servants. He even ate in the water. His diet consisted mainly of beef, lamb and, you've guessed it, water.

Roche, Sir Boyle (1743-1807)
This Irish MP came out with some 'Sam Goldwyn' style nuggets, including: 'Those who opposed freedom of speech should be silenced.'

Commenting on Ireland's loss of Parliament in the Act of Union in 1801 he said, 'It would surely be better to give up not only a part, but if necessary the whole of our Constitution to preserve the remainder.'

Didn't believe in doing anything for posterity because posterity 'never did anything for us.'

Thought the only way to prevent what was past was to put a stop to it before it happened.

Wrote the following to an acquaintance: 'I should have answered your letter a fortnight ago but I didn't receive it until this morning.'

Was once shown the body of a young man who'd been shot to death through the forehead. 'It was just as well the bullet didn't hit him between the eyes,' he remarked, 'or he might have lost his sight.'

Believed all wooden gates should be made of iron.

Believed that if people wrote anonymous letters, the least they should do is sign their names to them.

Ros, Amanda (1860-1939)
A strong contender for the worst writer of all time, County Down's Amanda had nonetheless a huge faith in her talent. She began writing at a young age, showing a pronounce penchant for naming the characters in her works alliteratively. Over the next few decades she would create Osbert Otwell, Irene Iddesleiah, Barney Blocter, Goliath Ginbottle and Bishop Barelegs. She also evinced a strong desire to name her characters after foods, so we also get people like lilly Lentil, Madame Pear, Mrs Strawberry, Peter Plum and Christopher Currant.

She often mixed sentences up to refer to two different scenarios as in this one where she simultaneously writes about a patient and the person visiting him: 'On entering the chamber of sickness with a new bottle of medicine sent from London, Sir John raised himself slightly on his left elbow.'

Her style of writing ranged from breathy rhetoric to quasi-Biblical mumbo-jumbo. People often bought her books from a perverse excitement, just to see how bad they could be. The Oxford Amanda Ros Society was founded in her honour. Here the literati came to read her works and chortle merrily over their ghastliness.

Amanda, meanwhile, stayed blithely indifferent to her literary failings. Ignoring any comments about her that she didn't like, she told people she was uniformly adored, replying to her detractors by calling them 'evil-minded snapshots of spleen' and 'clay crabs of corruption.' (The alliteration, as can be seen, extended even beyond the books).

She ran into money problems in 1917 and had to convert the ground floor of her house into a shop. The man who took out the lease on it opened it on Sundays. This was against her religious principles so she did everything in her power to keep customers out of it, including putting a banner in the window that said, 'All Detractors of the Sabbath Shall be Punished.' (She seemed to forget that such detractors were helping to pay her rent).

Amanda contemplated applying for the Nobel Prize for Literature in 1930 but (mercifully) changed her mind at the last minute. When she died at the ripe old age of 78 the world still hadn't cottoned on to her genius.

Russell, George (1867-1964)
Was so annoyed at a printer for leaving out the first two letters of the word 'aeon' in a poem of his, decided o write under the pseudonym 'AE' for the rest of his life.

Ryan, George (1956-2010)
The late lamented broadcaster had some unusual habits, among them a quirk that didn't allow him to leave his work for house unless his bed was made.

Spoke on his radio show once about a man who broke into a health shop and stole the entire contents. Police, he said, were looking for someone between the ages of 17 and 85.

Saint Patrick
Ireland's patron saint may have been Welsh. Ian Paisley thought he was a Protestant. Terry Eagleton said, 'We don't really know who he was. There may have been two of him. And he may not have existed at all.'

Scally, Stephen
Has discovered that thirteen out of eery ten women prefer chocolate to Maths.

Scanlon, Anne-Marie
Describes herself as a romantic, but uneasily so. Once knew a girl whose parents fell in love beside a septic tank.

Says her idea of exercise is lighting a cigarette.

Shaw, George Bernard (1856-1950)
Often wrote at a rotating work shed in his garden in Ayot St. Lawrence to get the best out of the sun.

Conducted an epistolary romance with his friend Ellen Terry for 26 years before finally meeting her. Began one of his letters to her like this: 'Ellen, Ellen, Ellen, Ellen, Ellen, Ellen, Ellen, Eleanor, Eleanest.'

Was so upset to lose his virginity at 29 (to an elderly widow) he didn't attempt sexual relations with other women for another fifteen years.

Believed there was no satisfaction in hanging a man who didn't object to it.

Described his hobbies as 'Cycling and showing off.'

Left money in his will to be put towards the construction of a new, 44-word alphabet which would be phonetic. (He once spelt 'fish' 'ghoti' taking the 'gh' from trough, the 'o' from 'women' and the 'ti' from 'station.')

Sheen, Martin (1940-)
Assisted at the delivery of his second son... but mistook the placenta for his twin.

Shiels, Brush (1952-)
The singer says his favourite word is 'floccinaucinihilipilification.'

Sheridan, Jim (1949-)b
Won an Oscar nomination for directing My Left Foot in 1989. Said afterwards, 'My Left Foot went to my head.'

Once rang his brother Peter and said, 'How are ye? I can't remember what I rang you for. I'll ring back in a minute when I find out.'

Sheridan, Richard Brinsley (1751-1816)
Like many writers, was a heavy drinker. Would even take eau-de-cologne if nothing else was available.

After being informed by his doctor that his drinking threatened the 'coating' of his stomach, he said, 'Then my stomach must learn to digest the drink in its waistcoat.'

Asked a woman he liked to visit his garden because, as he said, his roses would like to see her.

When one of his servants dropped a trayful of plates with a ferocious din one day, he said, 'I hope you've broken some of them. I'd hate it if you made all that noise for nothing.'

Skeffington, Clothworthy, 2nd Earl of Massereene
This flamboyant peer loved shadow-boxing. When he landed a good blow on himself he'd flex his muscles and cry out, 'Sweet little Massa!'

Often dined on the roof of his house. When he did so, his servants had to hoist up chairs and tables on a pulley. Guests attended by climbing a ladder from the inside of the house. Sometimes changed his mind about this, cancelling the whole meal after people had hardly sat down, and had everything carried back down again.

Was so heartbroken over the death of his wife's dog that he had it buried in a lead coffin. He left instructions that all the dogs of the parish attend the funeral and that fifty of them be dressed in white scarfs.

Left all his estate to his widow. When his brothers discovered they were only getting a guinea each they contested the will, insisting the earl was insane. A court verdict reversed his wishes, not on grounds of his insanity but rather his wife's undue influence over him.

Spain, Karl
This comedian's life has been a lot easier for him since he discovered the phone book was alphabetical. That save him hours of looking up numbers.

Thinks Ireland's recession was a myth generated by the government to get rid of foreigners.

Believes in loving your enemies, 'just in case your friends turn out to be a heap of bastards.'

Feels there's no time like the present for postponing what you don't want to do.

Stapleton, Frank (1956-)
The former Irish international is reputed to be grumpy. According to Tony Cascarino, the first thing he does every morning is smile. To get it over with.

Said of a player once: 'He didn't get booked for the yellow card.'

Described another player as having 'a knock on the shin just above the knee.'

Stephens, Bill (1924-1953)
Most animal trainers work in circuses but his man kept his lions and lionesses in waste ground at the back of his house in Fairview. A fearsome individual, he sometimes fed them by putting meat in his mouth and letting them pull it from him.

One day in 1951 a lioness escaped as Stephens was feeding him and ran riot through Fairview in broad daylight. Amazingly, the local cinema had just shown a film called *Jungle Stampede*. People doing their shopping gaped in horror as the lioness attacked a petrol pump attendant and then ran into a field. Children scrambled onto walls for a better view. The police were called. Stephens pleaded with them not to shoot his beloved animal – who was also his livelihood – but then she attacked Stephens himself so she had to be shot. 'Once she had the taste of my blood,' he said, 'she was no good to me in the circus anymore.'

My former brother-in-law Bill Whelan, an indigenous Fairview dweller, recalls hearing the story being told around his house as he was growing up. How could such a thing happen on an ordinary street in an ordinary suburb? It beggared belief. Bill wondered how people weren't mauled by the lion. Hearing details of his escape made him nervous growing up. It made him think it could happen again with some other lion. Walking down the street now became potentially fraught with danger instead of something he looked forward to.

The story became news all over the world. Stephens looked to capitalise his unlikely fame. He wanted to get into an American circus with his wife Mai. Mai worked with snakes.

He became more daring in his escapades. He bought a dangerous lion, Pasha, and invited some talent scouts from America to watch him training him.

They arrived over in 1953. Stephens was anxious to put on a good display but Pasha wouldn't come out of his cage for some reason. He went in after him and Pasha attacked him, going for his jugular. Stephens died instantly.

The reason Pasha attacked him was because he didn't recognise his smell. Stephens had just bought a new suit for a wedding he was going to and he was wearing it.

Stephens, James (1880-1950)
Spent a few impoverished years in Paris as a young man. 'One can starve very well on French bread,' he concluded.

Stoney, Pockets (?-1840)
Contemporary of Zozimus who got his name from the fact that one of his shoulders was higher than the other, something his mother tried to correct by filling the pockets of his coat with stones on the high side. The HSE haven't seen fit to embrace this practice into its general manifesto.

Sullivan, Tom
This man looked so fat the day he got married, he said it was the only time in history when the priest who performed the ceremony thought the *groom* was pregnant.

Sweeney, Mary
Took a flight in a helicopter belonging to the British Army in 1978 at the age of 103.

Swift, Jonathan (1667-1745)
Was known as 'The Mad Parson' in the parish where he was rector due to his odd behaviour and attitudes. Was notoriously misogynistic, suggesting women were a species 'hardly a degree above a monkey.'

To gain money for the government, he proposed a tax on women's beauty. 'Let every woman be permitted to assess her own charms,' he said, 'Then she'll be generous enough.'

Had an obsession with numbers. Told acquaintances that the walk from his apartment in Chelsea to the centre of London was 5748 paces.

In his essay 'A Modest Proposal' he recommended that a good solution for Ireland's over-population problem was to cook and eat babies.

Said he once knew a man who was so anxious to sell his house, he carried a brick in his pocket and showed it to anyone he met as a sample.

One time he made a vow to stop talking to people for an entire year.

Was obsessed with exercise, imaging it would protect him from disease. Often walked up to ten miles a day. If it was raining he ran up and down his stairs repeatedly to warm up. In his later years he ate his meals while walking around the place.

Always told people he would die like a tree, 'from the top first.' This did come to pass. As his mind deteriorated, his manservants were cruel enough to charge people a fee to chortle at him in his dementia.

Left money in his will to be put towards a psychiatric hospital so maybe he had the last laugh at 'the mad Irish.' This was his self-composed epitaph:

'He gave what little wealth he had

To build a house for fools and mad
And showed by one satiric touch
No nation wanted it so much.'

Synge, John Millington (1871-1909)
The absent-minded author once played a song for his nephew on a violin. When it was over, the boy said, 'Uncle Johnnie, how did you make that noise?' Synge looked at him and said, 'Did I?'

Another time he asked a friend, 'What is a tea-pot?' (He never learned to make a cup of tea right through his life).

Thought he was psychic. After he had an operation on his throat he said to his friend Cherrie Haughton, 'I tried to send you a telepathic message before I went under the ether. Did you get it?' When she said she didn't he was disgusted.

Synon, Mary Ellen (1951-)
This journalist had to resign from the Sunday Independent after labelling the 2000 Paralympics in Sydney 'cripples', and the event itself 'grotesque'.

Some of her political ideas were equally weird. One of her suggestions to bring about a United Ireland was to sell the idea to Unionists as a 32-county Ulster.

Talbot, Matt (1856-1925)
Talbot was a building site hot carrier who drank too much before his 'Road to Damascus' experience at the age of 28 which resulted in him forswearing alcohol for the rest of his life. After his conversion he spent most of his free time on his knees in churches attempting to atone for his sins, and those of mankind in general. After he died a number of chains were found wound around his arms and legs. They'd

obviously been there a long time because they'd cut into his flesh.

Generally slept on a plank, with a wooden block for his head.

Taylor, Alice (1941-)
Taylor's grandmother retired to her bed every few years convinced she was going to die. If her doctor disagreed with her she grew disappointed and sought a second opinion.

Taylor, Dennis (1949-)
Taylor has a reputation as a wit as well as being a former world champion snooker player. When he applied for a job at a building site one time, the foreman asked him if he could make a cup of tea. He then asked him if he was able to drive a forklift. Taylor enquired, 'How big is the teapot?'

When a referred declared a 'touching ball' situation during a frame once, Taylor enquired, 'Are they *both* touching?'

Funds were so tight going dancing as a young man, he once shared a taxi with fourteen others.

The world snooker final of 1985 where he beat Steve Davis 18-17 pulled in over 18 million viewers. One man watching it actually got a heart attack and died. As soon as his family saw him laid out, they turned the television set back on to watch the final frame. 'We feel sure he would have approved,' they told neighbours who'd come to see the match. Another man announced at a vital stage, 'If Taylor wins this, I'll convert to Catholicism.' The following day he received a message of congratulations from an unusual source: It had been smuggled out of Long Kesh prison from an inmate's tooth.

Believes Steve Davis is so laidback he takes valium as a stimulant.

Thomas, Caitlin (1913-94)
Said she never really suffered from morning sickness when she was pregnant because she was so used to hangovers.

Teirnan, Tommy (1969-)
Is a native of Navan, 'a town that's spelt the same backwards for a reason.'

Went into a restaurant one day in America and asked for a newspaper. The person serving him said, 'Would you like cheese with that?'

Thinks Hitler got the idea for the goosestep from his mother bringing him to Irish dancing classes when he was growing up.

Got death threats after saying Hitler should have killed more Jews for the gold in their teeth.

His father used to open the Obituary page in the paper and go, 'Right, let's see who gave up smoking yesterday.'

Says he's so self-critical he could almost sue himself for defamation of character.

Wouldn't have a problem shooting the Pope 'because I know he'd forgive me.'

Doesn't think a suicide bomber would work well in Ireland. 'He'd be there with a bale of briquettes under his jacket looking for a light.'

His son pronounces popcorn 'cockporn.' Which, he says, makes it a bit embarrassing when he's ordering it in a cinema.

Toibin, Niall (1929-2019)
As a Corkman, he once said he was nostalgic for his home town even when he was in it.

Used to frequent a restaurant in Cork which had a sign that said, 'Eat here and you'll never eat anywhere else again.'

Knew a man who was asked if it was true that the Irish always answered one question with another. 'Who told you that?' he enquired.

Townsend, Andy (1963-)
When asked what part of Ireland he came from, replied, 'South London.'

Lists the most embarrassing moment of his life when Jack Charlton farted in front of Albert Reynolds and blamed it on him.

Treacy, Ray (1946-2015)
Eamon Dunphy said he got 56 caps for Ireland, 'but 30 of those were for his singing.'

Trevor, Williams (1928-)
At the PEN Literary Award ceremony in 2002 he stood up and said, 'I hold the record for the world's shortest speech and I don't want to ruin my reputation. Good night.'

Tubridy, Ryan (1973-)
Claims to have a good face for radio.

Twink (1951-)

Her mother was so quiet, she thought she was adopted: 'How could such a ladylike little woman have given birth to a volcano?'

Her life has had some unusual coincidences. She wanted to buy a fur coat once in London but couldn't afford the price the shop was asking. A few minutes after coming out of it, she saw a taxi about to run into a woman on the street. She pulled the woman back onto the pavement, probably saving her life. It turned out she was the manager of the shop. To reward her, she sold her the coat at a huge cut.

Another coincidence happened when she was appearing in a play in which had to smoke. She suffered from asthma so the director gave her herbal cigarettes. Unfortunately, they smelled like marijuana and audiences complained that she was smoking dope. As a last resort she tried menthol cigarettes but they caused her tongue to swell. She went to an orthodontist to see if he could help. As she was waiting to be attended by him, she started reading the magazines in his waiting-room. One of them had an interview with Farrah Fawcett-Majors. In it she talked about being in a play once where she had to smoke menthol cigarettes. Which caused her tongue to swell. And to result in her having to go to an orthodontist...

Was interviewed by Gay Byrne on the morning of her wedding.

Wants to be buried with her dogs.

Walkington, D.B. (1867-1926)
Walkington was a rugby fullback who lined out for Ireland eight times in the 1880s. What distinguished him from the other players was the fact that he wore a monocle even on the pitch, taking it out and polishing it before he took free kicks.

Well, Jim
South Down politician faced with a thorny situation in 2009: A fire station in Rathfriland was gutted... because it hadn't been fitted with a smoke alarm.

Whaley, Buck (1766-800)
Profligate son of Richard Chapell Whaley, a Protestant Irish landowner and magistrate who left him £60,000 in his will as well as a steady income of £7000 a year from all his assets. Buck did his best to spend this in record time. He was sent to Paris at the age of 16 but had to leave after incurring huge gambling debts - £14,000 from one night's flurries alone.

In Dublin he wagered a bet of £15,000 that he'd go to Jerusalem and back within two years. He won that one. Another bet required him to jump from his drawing room window onto the first passenger carriage that passed by and kiss its female occupant if there was one. This he also achieved with some aplomb.

Proposed marriage to a young Belfast woman he'd never seen in his life before. She was merely admiring his house one day so he popped the question. Perhaps wisely, she declined his offer.

Whatley, Archbishop Richard (1800-90)
This Dublin Archbishop used to keep himself trim by swimming from the branches of trees even in his old age.

Couldn't sit still. While telling stories he would bend his right leg, grab the foot with his left hand and tug at it repeatedly to stretch the joints. Afterwards he usually whirred himself around on whatever chair he was sitting, balancing them on two legs, or even one. He broke dozens of them like this. He was even known to put his foot into someone else's pocket in the middle of his gymnastics.

Didn't like people with flat heads, believing them to be untrustworthy. To decipher a person's true character he advised dropping a handful of peas onto their head. 'If a large number remain,' he'd say, 'tell the butler to lock up the plates.'

He had an original cure for headaches: Chop down a tree and then go to sleep.

Whelan, Marty (1956-)
Claims that commenting on the Eurovision Song Contest sometimes makes him lose the will to live.

Wilde, Oscar (1854-1900)
Asked once to name his hundred favourite books he replied, 'I can't – I've only written five.'

Wilde was suffering from depression one day, so much so that when an acquaintance asked him what was wrong with him, he blurted out, 'It is said. One half of the world does not believe in God, and the other half doesn't believe in me.'

Said of a performance of a dramatic work he wrote, 'The play was a success, but the audience a total failure.'

Went into a florist's shop one day and asked for a flower to be taken out of the window. The florist asked him, 'Which one would you like, sir?' He replied, 'I don't want to buy one. I just thought some of them looked a little tired sitting there.'

Another day Oscar looked very pale over the breakfast table. Asked what was wrong with him, he said he'd been up all night tending a sick primrose he'd picked in a wood the previous day.

When he was asked if he knew George Moore he replied, 'Know him? I know him so well I haven't spoken to him for ten years.'

After being arrested for homosexuality, he was upset by the rough treatment accorded to him by his jailers. 'If this is the way the Queen treats her prisoners,' he droned, 'then she doesn't deserve to have any.'

A woman he knew came up to him in the street once and shook his hand warmly. When she realised he hadn't a clue who she was she said, 'My name is Smith.' Wilde replied, 'I remember your name perfectly. It's your face I can't think of.'

Wilkinson, Colm T. (1944-)
After Wilkinson landed the part of Judas in Jesus Christ Superstar his mother refused to speak to him for six months. 'Anyone but him,' she accused.

Wogan, Terry (1938-2016)
Was so terrified of becoming a priest that he prayed he *wouldn't* get a vocation.

On the 20th anniversary of his marriage, wrote a card to his wife saying, 'Happy anniversary to a woman who hasn't changed since our wedding day. Iron your face and I'll take you out on the town. Love, Ter.'

On his gravestone he wanted the following words to be written: 'He didn't know what he was doing.'

Yeats, William Butler (1865-1939)
Celebrated winning the Nobel Prize for Literature in 1923 by eating sausages.

Had this to say about Seamus O'Sullivan: 'The only trouble with him is that when he's not drunk he's sober.'

Had his head in the clouds so much, often he didn't recognise his own children. Passed his daughter Anne in the street one day and enquired of her, 'Pray, child, what is your name?'

Frank O'Connor said he'd often be in the middle of conversation when he'd suddenly break off and start beating time with his hands as he recited one of his poems. Then he'd go back to the conversation as if nothing happened.

When asked how he planned to choose his actors for the Abbey he said, 'I will go into the audition room and put everyone's name on a sheet of paper. I will then put the pieces of paper into a hat and draw out the first twelve.'

Was so besotted with Maud Gonne MacBride he gushed, 'If she said the world was flat I would still be proud to be of her party.' Repeatedly proposed marriage to her and was repeatedly rejected. The one time she did agree to marry him he said, no. He then changed his mind, but so did she. In later years her daughter Iseult proposed to him but he refused because their horoscopes were incompatible. After Maud Gonne's last rejection of him he was sufficiently mollified to accept Iseult's proposal but by then she too had changed her mind. (It ran in the family).

Had an operation in 1934 that promised to rejuvenate ageing men by the implantation of new sex glands. When he was asked his reasons for having it, he offered the enlightening: 'I fall asleep after lunch!'

Patrick Campbell's wife Beatrice was acting in one of his plays at the Abbey and was always fascinated by his meditations. During rehearsals one day she asked him what he was thinking about. 'I'm thinking,' he said, 'of the master of a wayside Indian railway station who sent a message to his company's headquarters saying, 'Tigress On The Line. Wire Instructions.'

Put sugar in his soup and salt in his coffee. One day Brendan Behan's mother served him parsnips. He sniffed them and said, 'That is a very peculiar pudding.'

During the production of a play once, he noticed a red glow at the back of the stage. He said, 'That's exactly what I want for the sunset scene.' At this point an electrician appeared. 'I'm afraid you'll have to wait till tomorrow, sir,' he said, 'The theatre's on fire.'

Towards the end of his life Oliver St. John Gogarty said of him, 'Yeats has now reached the age where he can't take yes for an answer.'

Young, Dusty
A gay burglar broke into his house one night, he said, and re-arranged the furniture.

There were so many shotgun weddings at his local church, it was eventually dubbed 'Winchester Cathedral.'

Knew a man who had a vasectomy by mistake. He went in to hospital to have his tonsils out and someone turned the trolley round.

Claimed his father died from drink and sex: 'He couldn't get either so he shot himself.'

Came to Dublin recently for his father's 103rd birthday but he wasn't there. He died at 36.

Zozimus
Born in 1794 as Michael Moran, Zozimus, as he came to be known (he took the name from a fifth century cleric) was blinded a few months after his birth. He became an itinerant storyteller who wandered around the streets of Dublin in a long frieze coat, a brown beaver hat, corduroy trousers and a blackthorn stick tied to his wrist by a leather thong. He recited doggerel poetry of his own composition to all and sundry, stopping every few minutes for donations. He has become immortalised in the Irish folk memory as one of its legendary street characters because of his lovable passion for corny lines. He died in 1846.